We care for the Ch

The Chiltern Society aims to conserve the beauty and character of the Chiltern Hills. Since being founded in 1965, the Society has made a significant contribution to the quality of life as we know it today in the Chilterns. With well over 6,000 members, it has become one of the largest regional conservation groups in the country.

The Chiltern Way was originally conceived as the Society's project to celebrate the Millennium: a bold initiative to encourage more walkers to explore and enjoy the beauty of the Chiltern Hills.

It has involved much research to identify the best long distance circular walk to include some of the most beautiful countryside. Many hours have been spent opening up little used footpaths and bridleways, organising and erecting over 2,000 signs, liaising with local owners and publicising the walk. All this has been done by Chiltern Society volunteers who generously give freely of their time. Nevertheless a project this size does incur considerable expenditure. Most of this has been donated by members of the Society and Chiltern Way Founder Member status has been granted to all our major donors whose names are recorded in this book unless they have expressed a wish to remain anonymous. Many Local Authorities have also supported our project with donations and their names are also listed.

We are most grateful for all this enthusiastic support and also for the generous contributions from our sponsors whose advertisements appear in the next few pages.

We hope this project will give much pleasure to many and encourage a better understanding and appreciation of the Chilterns. We hope that any readers who are not already members of the Chiltern Society will wish to obtain further information as indicated on the last page of this book.

Michael Rush, Chairman of the Chiltern Society (1997–   )

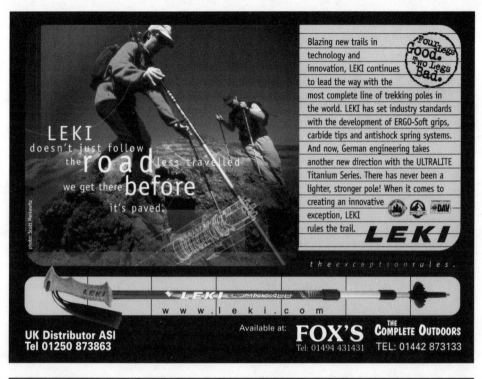

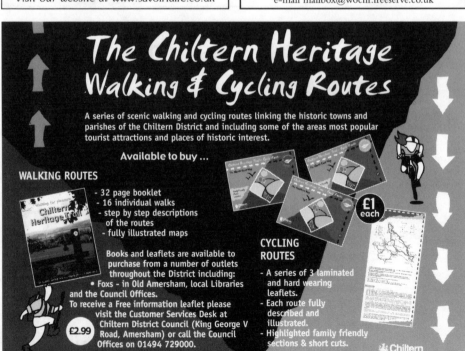

FOUNDER MEMBERS
OF THE CHILTERN WAY

The Chiltern Society is most grateful to all those who have made generous donations towards the cost of the Chiltern Way Project

Raymund & Margaret Adcock
Mrs Margaret Adnitt
Rosemarie Aldridge
Peter Allen
Richard & Frances Allsop
Mr & Mrs C D Allsop
Robin Allum
John Andrew
Sir John & Lady Anson
Armytage family
Mr & Mrs T Ashcroft
Pat Atkin
Nick Atkins
Frank & Heather Auton
Nigel & Ann Aylesbury

Mrs Pamela Bacon
Dr A H J Baines
Robert & Margaret Balding
Tony Balfour
Mr & Mrs K Ball
Mrs S P Ballard
Jim Banville
Robert Barber & Jaine McCormack
D R Barbour
John M Bargman
Brian & Margaret Barnes
Dr G W Barnett
Imogen, Vicky & Eamonn Barrett
Christopher Barry

Peter & Sheila Bartlett
Colin & Lorraine Bateman
John Beech OBE
Jim Bell
Colin Bendall
R & K Benson
Eileen Berry
Rob & Ann Bethell
Mrs Mary Bickerton
Alan & Susan Biddle
Alan Binder
Kitty Bird
Angela Bishop
A P Black
Mr A Blaney
Mary Blears
Judith Blofeld
K H Bond
D Bonwitt
Grattan Bowen
Hilda Bowerman
Anne and Michael Bowker
Bill Braham
Alfred & Frances Bramley
G A Brand
Guy Bratt
Clive & Jean Bray
Breachwood Green Society
Simon Bridbury
Philip Briers

Imogen Bright
Susan Brinn
Yvonne Bristow
B A Brockes
Don Brooks
Mrs Daphne Brooks
Rowan Brown
Mr & Mrs M Browning
Rowland & Judith Buck
M & J E Bullas
Mr & Mrs B Burrows
Pip & Gill Burston
Jeremy John Burton
Malcolm & Ann Busby
Delia M Butcher
Gregory Button

Tom Carpenter
Jim Casper & Jane Slater
Edward & Stella Casson
Martin Gray Chadwick
Colin Chadwick
Mr & Mrs R E Challinor
C A Chandler
Martyn Chant
Antony Chapman
Mrs M N Chassay
Douglas Chester
Mr & Mrs C Chown
John & Michele Christensen
Malcolm Christie
J A & I Churchill
Paul & Maureen Clark
David Clark
Kenneth Clarke

Michael Close
Don, Rosemarie & Christopher Collier
Mrs Lucy Collings
R D & S H Connor
Nigel Conradi
Catherine Cooksey
John Coombe
Miss P M Coombs
Kevin Corrigan
Mr & Mrs T Cotton
R D Coulson
Jennifer & Warwick Cowan
The Crawford family
Mrs E E Crawford-Condie
David Cripps
Elspeth Crossman
Alan Crowe
Marie Crowhurst
Elizabeth Cruickshank
Mrs Margaret Crush
P Cullen

Mr & Mrs N W Darkins
Mr & Mrs D R Davies
Mrs Andrew Davis
Mrs M Davison
Tina Day
Mike and Anne Dean
Mr A del Tufo
Sir John Dellow
P M C Denby
Shiela A Denham
John & Wendy Denison
David Dennis & Lesley Paton

J G Dewes
Geoff Dewhurst
Gerald Dickerson
Stephanie Diggon
The Dixon family
Penny Dole
Geoff & Janet Donnelly
Rosemary Donnelly
Dorothy Drew
Julia Drummond
Elaine Du Lieu
Richard Du Plessis
Mrs S J Duncan
Tony Duparc
H W & J Dupree
Ron & Kathy Durnford
Ian Durrell
Marion Durrell

David East
Canon John Eastgate
Ian & Anne Eastwood
R & M Edwards
Mr & Mrs G J Edwards
E J Eele
David & Jeanne-Hélène Eggleton
Eileen Eldridge
B A Ellison

Christine Fairburn
Jane Faulkner
J P A Fenley
Sylvia Fennimore
Sir Leonard Figg
R Filmer

Ray Flanigan
Russell Fleming
Trevor Fletcher & Heather Kent
Dr & Mrs David Flynn
Chris K Folland
Ian & Hilary Forbes
Bridget M Forbes
Stuart Fordyce
Janice Foster
Mr & Mrs T H Fowler
Judy & Stephen Fox
Mike & Jacki Fox
Mrs A Fox
Edward W G France
Marion Francis
Mrs A M Frank
Mrs D Fry

John & Meryl Gardner
John & Katharine Garrow
Peter & Jean Gell
Ruth J Gibbins
Eric Gibbs
Mr A E H Gilbert
Margaret Gladwin
Amis & Meg Goldingham
Bob Goodspeed
Donald & Julie Gough
Mr & Mrs D Govier
Maximin E Green
Jill Greenfield
Guy Greenhous
Jim & Carole Griffin
Michael Grimer
Mr & Mrs D A T Grimmett

The Grotefeld family
Andrew J Gunz
Jean Gustavson

H Hakimzadeh & F Ebtehaj
R J Hall
David Hankinson
The Happy Wanderers Walking Club
Peter Harden
Joan Hardie
Cyril Harding
Bee Hardy
Mrs D M Hargreaves
Stephen Harris
Martyn Hart
Mr John Hauxwell F.I.B.M.
Anthony & Margaret Hawes
Bob Hawkins
Brian Hawkins
Hazlemere Residents Association
Lorna Head
Ronald Heath
Mrs Heather Herrington
Kath Hester
Richard G Hill
Roger Hill
John Hill
Paul & Janet Hilton
Audrey Hind
Michael Hobkirk
Harry Hodson & Joan Curci
Mrs Ruth M Haines (nee Hofer)
David J Hofer
Peter M Hofer

Mr & Mrs John F Hofer
Mayke Hogestijn & Christer Klingwall
John & Gloria Holmes
Mr J C Holt
Susan Hopkins
Paddy Hopkirk
John & Monica Hornsey
Valerie Horsburgh
Glen Horwood
Leslie Hubbard
D & B Hughes
Mr A J Hughes
Joe Hughes
Mrs Celia Humphrey
Beryl Hunt
K C Huxham

Mr D Ibell
Tony Ibotson
C P & P A Iliffe
Mrs Karen Ilott

Mr K H Jackson
M Jackson
D S Jackson
Margaret Jakeman
R C Janes
Mr Tom & Mrs Susan Jellis

Laurie Jennings
Sir John Johnson
Brian & Eileen Johnson
Bryan Jones
Penny Jones

Joan & Maurice Jones
Simon & Jo Kearey
Sheila Keatinge
Peter Keen
E R Kendrick
Ben Kent
Cheryl & David Kent
The Kent & Caldecourt families
Mr & Mrs Timothy Keown
Elizabeth Kerry
David King
Peter King
R M King
Nikki King
Clifford King OBE
Neil & Wendy Kingon
Oliver S Knowles

D M Ladd
A Christopher Lake
Beryl Lant
David Leah
D O Leary
D N Ledeboer
Chris & Susan Lee
Mrs F M Lefebure
Margaret Legg
L W Legg
Michael Leon
Angela & Adrian Lepper
Dennis Lewington
Roger & Vivien Lewis
Richard Lewis
Brenda Liddiard
David Lindsey

Patricia Lindsley
Austin & Hilary Little
Peter J Lugg
Heather Lund
Leslie Lunn
Mr & Mrs R B Lyle

Mrs Shirley Macara
Brian G Machin
Donald & Sally Main
Colin Maloney
Colin Mansfield
Jean Marsh
Alan & Stella Marsh
John & Maureen Marsh
Allan Marshall
G D & C Martin
Wing Cdr Derek Martin OBE
Mr & Mrs R Martin-Fagg
Trevor and Mary Marwood
John Mason
Sharon McCullough & David Robso
George McFarlane
Shirley Mckiernon
Peter & Joan McLoughlin
Mrs McNeile
Mr & Mrs McNicoll
Eric & Muriel Meadows
George H Messenger
Jean Middlemiss
Janet Mahala Miles
Don & Diana Millar
C H Mitchell
David S Mitchell
Peter Mogford

Gwyn & Elizabeth Morgan
Mr & Mrs F T Morrell
C J E & A R W Morris
Susan & Richard Morris
Harry & Diana Mullens

Mr H B Naish
David & Susan Nash
John Naylor-Smith
John Neiger
Douglas Nethercleft
Hans H Neustadt
Edward & Gerda Newmark
John Nicholls
David Nobbs
Dr & Mrs T J Nokes
North West London Ramblers'
Group
Tony Northwood
Paul & Venetia Nye

Pamela Oakford
The Ody family of Bourne End
Cherry Ohajuru
Bob & Cheryll Older
C & D Oram
Ross & Jane Osborn
Neil Oughtred

Mr & Mrs C J Palmer
Mr & Mrs Q Palmer
Mr D V Palmer
Ann Paris
Charles G A Parker
David Pascall

Jim Patterson
Louise Pearl
Martin Pedler
Barbara Peerman
Joyce Pendry
Penn & Tylers Green Society
Geoffrey Perfect
John & Patricia Perfect
Alan & Liz Perks
Alan Phear
P A T Phibbs
Richard Phillips
Mr & Mrs T F Phillips
Dr Ian H Pike
Mrs P S Pim
Mrs R J Pither
Mungo Pitman
A R Platts
Mr & Mrs Charles Pocock
C G Pocock
Gillian Pole
Pat & John Porter
Margaret & Geoffrey Potts
Mrs Adeline E Pratt
Chris Pratt
Tony Price
Peter & Una Prior
Lily Protter
John & Maureen Purdy
Thomas & Edward Purkhardt
Mr & Mrs A J R Pursell

Brian & Isabella Rance
R C (Brokers)
Albin John Reed

John & Beryl Reeves
Elizabeth & Michael Reupke
John Reuter
L M & S R Richardson
Mavis & Alun Roberts
Mr P G Roberts
Ian & Diane Roberts
Leslie Robins
S F Robinson
J Alan Robinson
Owen Robinson
Roy K B Roe
John M Roper
B J & S A Rowan
John Rowe
Robin & Val Rowland
Michael & Linda Rush

Peter Sachs
Philip Sadler
Neil Saunders
Martin Sayers
Shirley & Brian Scrivener
Trustees of Shekinah Trust
Mrs Jennifer E Sherwood
Joyce A Shiner
Mrs A Shooter
Colin J Simmons
Peter Simpson
Diana & Bob Simpson
Ronald L Sims
A A & S A Sipson
Carol & Eric Slater
D J Slaughter
H G Sledmere

James Smillie
Mr & Mrs Bernard Smith
Dilys Smith
Mr R C C Smith
Ken Smith
Keith E O Smith
Sheri Smith
Maggie Smith
S R Smith
Eileen Smith
Les & Ivy Smith
Don Snoad
Mr P D & Mrs J Somerville
Roland Spence
Roy & Sally Spencer
John D Spicer
Jane Squire
Ms Lynne Stainthorpe
Paul G Stamp
David Stark
Oliver Statham
Mr & Mrs P N Stoakley
Freddy Stokes
R A Stonell
Mr & Mrs Howard Storer
Mrs J Streeter
Mr & Mrs P M Sturges
Charles Surrey
Don & Sue Sutton
Robin Swain
Anne Symons

Shirley A Tarbox
David H Tarn
Roger Taylor

Mrs Jeannette Taylor
Dr David S Taylor
Heather & John Taylor
Paul Telford
Maggie and Bruin Templeman
J B Thomas
Mary & Grant Thomson
Alan & Sarah Tierney
Jean Timms
Joyce Tory
David Tracey
Mr & Mrs E Trott
Alan & Virginia Turner

Derek & Cic Upcott
Donald C Urry
Elizabeth & Tony Usher

David & Pat Varney

Carole A Wadlow
Ray & Jenny Wainwright
Commander Brian Wainwright OBE RN
Peter Wakeling
R C D Walker
Miss S M Walker
Professor & Mrs W D Wall
Lawrence Waller
Peggy Vannoy Walsh
Dr Vernon & Mrs Lynne Ward
Roger & Pam Ward, Chesham
Russell & Joyce Warner
Watford & District H F Rambling Club

I K Watson
Alastair & Basia Watson-Gandy
Lady Wellington
Simon Wennberg & Eunice Michaels
Mark & Elaine West
Anthony Wethered
E G Wheater
Mrs D M White
D J White
Linda Whitnall
J S Whyte CBE
Pauline Wilkinson
Mr & Mrs R Wilkinson
Sally Williams
Michael Wilson
Henry & Denise Wilson
Sqn Ldr J H Witherow & Mrs J M Witherow
Mr & Mrs D W Witton
Mrs B M Wood
Inge & Michael Woolf
Bob Woolley
George & Jo Worrall
Sir Denis Wright GCMG
Mary Wyeth

Mr C G Young
J S Young
David & Wendy Young
Mrs M J Young & Dr P Brodrick

LOCAL AUTHORITY SUPPORTERS

Bucks County Council

Herts County Council

Dacorum County Council

Aldbury Parish Council

Berkhamsted Town Council

Chalfont St Giles Parish Council
Chalfont St Peter Parish Council
Chinnor Parish Council
Chorleywood Parish Council
Coleshill Parish Council

Dunstable Town Council

Eaton Bray Parish Council
Ellesborough Parish Council
Ewelme Parish Council

Great & Little Hampden Parish
Council
Great Marlow Parish Council

Houghton Regis Town Council

Ibstone Parish Council

Lacey Green Parish Council

Nettlebed Parish Council

Northchurch Parish Council

Penn Parish Council

Radnage Parish Council
Redbourn Parish Council
Rotherfield Greys Parish Council
Rotherfield Peppard Parish
Council

Sarratt Parish Council
Stokenchurch Parish Council
Streatley Parish Council
Studham Parish Council
Sundon Parish Council

Toddington Parish Council
Tring Parish Council
Turville Parish Council

Watlington Parish Council
Wendover Parish Council
Wigginton Parish Council

We are also grateful to
'Millennium Festival Awards
For All'

The
Chiltern Way

A 200km circular walk
round the Chilterns

Nick Moon

The Chiltern Society

THE CHILTERN WAY

A Guide to this new 133-mile circular Long-Distance Path through Bedfordshire, Buckinghamshire, Hertfordshire & Oxfordshire.

Nick Moon

The Chiltern Way has been established by the Chiltern Society to mark the Millennium by providing walkers in the twenty-first century with a new way of exploring the diverse, beautiful countryside which all four Chiltern counties have to offer. Based on the idea of the late Jimmy Parsons´ Chiltern Hundred but expanded to cover the whole Chilterns, the route has largely been devised by the author and is being signposted, waymarked and improved by the Society´s Rights of Way Group in preparation for the Way´s formal launch in October 2000.

In addition to a description of the route and points of interest along the way, this guide includes 29 specially drawn maps of the route indicating local pubs, car parks, railway stations and a skeleton road network and details are provided of the Ordnance Survey and Chiltern Society maps covering the route.

The author, Nick Moon, has lived in or regularly visited the Chilterns all his life and has, for over 25 years, been an active member of the Chiltern Society´s Rights of Way Group, which seeks to protect and improve the area´s footpath and bridleway network. Thanks to the help and encouragement of the late Don Gresswell MBE, he was introduced to the writing of books of walks and has since written or contributed to a number of publications in this field.

OTHER PUBLICATIONS BY NICK MOON

Chiltern Walks Trilogy
Chiltern Walks 1:   Hertfordshire, Bedfordshire and
                       North Buckinghamshire:
                       Book Castle (new edition) 1996
Chiltern Walks 2 :   Buckinghamshire:
                       Book Castle (new edition) 1997
Chiltern Walks 3 :   Oxfordshire and West Buckinghamshire:
                       Book Castle (new edition) 1996

Family Walks
Family Walks 1 :   Chilterns - South : Book Castle 1997
Family Walks 2 :   Chilterns - North : Book Castle 1998

Oxfordshire Walks
Oxfordshire Walks 1: Oxford, The Cotswolds and The Cherwell
                     Valley: Book Castle (new edition) 1998
Oxfordshire Walks 2: Oxford, The Downs and The Thames Valley:
                     Book Castle 1995

The d´Arcy Dalton Way across the Oxfordshire Cotswolds and
                       Thames Valley : Book Castle 1999

Other Complete Books
Walks for Motorists: Chilterns (Southern Area):
                      Frederick Warne 1979
Walks for Motorists: Chilterns (Northern Area):
                      Frederick Warne 1979
Walks in the Hertfordshire Chilterns: Shire 1986

First published October 2000
by The Book Castle
12 Church Street, Dunstable, Bedfordshire.

Printed in Great Britain by Antony Rowe Ltd., Chippenham, Wilts.

ISBN 1 871 199 79 4

Contents

Cover photograph : Approaching Chalfont St. Giles (Section 3)
© Nick Moon

Introduction

The Chiltern Way, which has been created by the Chiltern Society as its Millennium project, is based on the idea of the late Jimmy Parsons' 'Chiltern Hundred`, but, whereas Jimmy's route was confined to a 100-mile circuit of the central Chilterns, the Chiltern Way takes in all four Chiltern counties in a 133-mile circuit extending from Ewelme, Oxfordshire in the southwest to Sharpenhoe Clappers, Bedfordshire and Great Offley, Hertfordshire in the northeast as well as going as far southeast as Chorleywood West on the Chiltern downslope. While this route does not attempt to follow the area boundary, not reaching the extremities of Caversham and Goring, Hitchin and Whitwell or Denham and Burnham Beeches, and equally some attractive areas of the interior are not visited, it does offer a good cross-section of the various types of characteristic Chiltern scenery.

Starting from Hemel Hempstead Station in Hertfordshire near the confluence of the Rivers Gade and Bulbourne, (which proved to be the nearest railway station to a route conceived as a circuit without a specific starting point), the Way leads you southwards over the Bovingdon plateau to Sarratt Church, before crossing a scenic section of the Chess valley and reaching the picturesque Buckinghamshire village of Chenies. You then continue southwards skirting Chorleywood to reach Newland Park where you can visit the Chiltern Open Air Museum with its collection of historic buildings and artefacts.

Now turning west, the Way descends into the Misbourne valley at the photogenic village of Chalfont St. Giles, where it briefly joins the South Bucks Way before continuing westwards across quiet upland in the Penn Country, passing north of Hodgemoor Wood to reach the traditional hilltop villages of Coleshill and Winchmore Hill. Turning southwestwards, you now pass through Penn Bottom and Penn itself to reach the Wye valley at Loudwater at a point where the preservation of the ancient common meadow of King's Mead as a recreation ground enables you to cross this otherwise very industrialised valley with a minimum of urban intrusion.

The Way then skirts Flackwell Heath to reach the upper northern slopes of the Thames Valley with wide views across it in places before passing through extensive woodland to skirt Marlow by way of Burroughs Grove, Marlow Bottom and Bovingdon Green. Here the Way turns west across the quiet wooded hills above the Thames Valley before descending into Hambleden and its valley, one of the jewels of the Chilterns and the lowest point on the Chiltern Way.

Now turning north, the Way leads you up the Hambleden Valley to Skirmett, before crossing a wooded hill which affords some fine views and descending to Fingest and Turville, two more villages whose photogenic character makes them favourite locations for calendar pictures and filming. Turning southwest again, the Way climbs with fine views to a high ridge at Southend Common and entering Oxfordshire, takes one of the most beautiful Chiltern paths, descending through woodland and Stonor Park with its magnificent house of mediæval origin to the estate village of Stonor.

Continuing westwards, the Way climbs with more fine views to cross the Oxfordshire Way at Maidensgrove, once described as 'perhaps the most remote hamlet in all the Chilterns` and skirt Russell's Water Common, before dropping into the heavily-wooded Bix Bottom with its nature reserve. From here, a short cut to Russell's Water village enables you to cut 10 miles off the route or take a 10-mile circular walk to and from Ewelme, while the main route continues westwards, crossing another high ridge at Park Corner, then descending through woodland and crossing the Ridgeway to reach an ancient road from Henley to Oxford. Having crossed Harcourt Hill with its wide views across the Thames Valley and Oxfordshire Plain, the Way then reaches its southwestern extremity at the picturesque, historic village of Ewelme with its ancient buildings and watercress beds.

Now turning eastwards, another open ridge with superb views is crossed, before a path recently added to the Definitive Map leads you to the top of Swyncombe Down, one of the most spectacular projections of the Chiltern escarpment. The Way then continues along the ridge before turning south onto the Ridgeway to reach Swyncombe with its 1000-year-old church. Leaving the Ridgeway, the Way then turns east to cross the main escarpment ridge at Cookley Green, before turning northeast across the upper reaches of a series of typical heavily-wooded ridges and bottoms at the back of the escarpment, passing through Russell's Water, Pishill Bottom and Northend and recrossing the Oxfordshire Way at Hollandridge. From Northend, descending steeply through woodland to reenter Buckinghamshire, you reach the beautiful Wormsley Valley, where an ancient estate succeeded in excluding public roads, before crossing another high ridge at Ibstone to reach Stokenchurch, one of the highest villages in the Chilterns, which, despite its unfortunate reputation as the 'ugly duckling of the Chilterns`, is a superb centre for walking in the surrounding hills.

Continuing northeastwards with fine views, a series of ridges and bottoms in the Radnage area are crossed before you climb up Bledlow Ridge. Turning northwards, the Way then descends, crossing the Ridgeway west of Lodge Hill and several low ridges to reach Bledlow at the foot of the escarpment, then turns east across the Risborough gap in the escarpment, visiting Saunderton, recrossing the Ridgeway and climbing to Lacey Green with its restored seventeenth-century windmill. From here, the Way leads you northeastwards across the heavily-wooded uplands of the Hampden Country, following parts of Grim´s Ditch, visiting Great Hampden, home of the leading Parliamentarian soldier, crossing Hampden Bottom and reaching the remote upland hamlet of Little Hampden, where you once again join the South Bucks Way.

Leaving the South Bucks Way again at Cobblers Hill, the Chiltern Way continues northeastwards, crossing the dry upper reaches of the Misbourne valley and another somewhat less wooded range of quiet uplands by way of Lee Gate, Buckland Common, a further section of Grim´s Ditch and Wigginton to reach the Bulbourne valley and Grand Union Canal at Cow Roast. Now back in Hertfordshire, the Way heads for Aldbury with some fine views across the Tring Gap, before climbing to cross the heavily-wooded Ashridge Estate to reach Little Gaddesden, then descends into the Gade valley, entering Bedfordshire. Turning north, the Way now crosses another range of uplands, passing through Studham and skirting Whipsnade Wild Animal Park and Tree Cathedral, before emerging onto the top of the Dunstable Downs, where the Way reaches its highest point and superb views abound.

From here, the Way begins the circling of the Luton/Dunstable conurbation, which forms its most northerly section, descending to cross the ancient Icknield Way on the edge of Dunstable, then crossing a series of open Chiltern foothills with extensive views in places, passing through Sewell, Bidwell and Chalton. Having crossed the M1, the Way then climbs onto the most northerly ridge of the Chilterns at Upper Sundon and follows it by way of Sundon Hills Country Park to Sharpenhoe Clappers with an abundance of panoramic views, passing a number of spectacular steep-sided coombes. Leaving the escarpment, the Way then turns southeast, passing through Streatley and heading for the open downs of Galley Hill and Warden Hill, where more panoramic views open out across Luton and the hills to the east. Now turning east, the Way soon reenters Hertfordshire and passes through the former estate village of Lilley, before turning south through the surprisingly quiet hills east of Luton, eventually crossing the southeastern tip of Bedfordshire and the Lea valley at East Hyde to reenter Hertfordshire on the edge of the dormitory town of Harpenden.

The final 12 miles of the Way, then lead you westwards through quiet hills to recross the M1 and reach the hilltop village of

Flamstead, before turning southwestwards through remote hill country to cross the Gade valley at the picturesque hamlet of Water End. You now cross one final ridge at Potten End to enter Hemel Hempstead by way of one of its 'green lungs' and return to your starting point.

While the full 133-mile route can be completed by the more energetic in a week or less or, in a more leisurely fashion, in up to a fortnight or can be split into a series of one-day walks, a whole range of shorter variations are also possible. For example, the 10-mile Ewelme loop can be omitted or the South Bucks Way or Grand Union Canal towpath or both can be used to cut across from the northbound to the southbound section of the Way or vice versa, while parts of the western section can be walked together with the parallel part of the Ridgeway. These and other alternative options can be identified by consulting the overview map on pages 10/11.

As the availability of overnight accommodation varies from year to year, it is advisable to contact a local tourist information centre for up-to-date information and bookings. These are as follows:-

Amersham (seasonal)   : 01494-729492
Dunstable   : 01582-471012
Hemel Hempstead   : 01442-234222
Henley-on-Thames   : 01491-578034
High Wycombe   : 01494-421892
Luton   : 01582-401579
Marlow   : 01628-483597
Thame   : 01844-212834
Wallingford   : 01491-826972
Wendover   : 01296-696759

Throughout its length, the Chiltern Way follows public rights of way, uses recognised permissive paths or crosses public open space. As the majority of paths used cross land used for economic purposes such as agriculture, forestry or the rearing of game, walkers are urged to follow the Country Code at all times:-

- Guard against all risk of fire
- Fasten all gates
- Keep dogs under proper control
- Keep to the paths across farmland
- Avoid damaging fences, hedges and walls
- Leave no litter - take it home
- Safeguard water supplies
- Protect wild life, wild plants and trees
- Go carefully on country roads on the right-hand side facing oncoming traffic
- Respect the life of the countryside

Observing these rules helps prevent financial loss to landowners and damage to the environment, as well as the all-too-frequent and sometimes justified bad feeling towards walkers in the countryside.

Details of possible parking places are given in the introductory information to each section and any convenient railway stations are shown on the accompanying plan. As bus services are liable to frequent change, including information in this book might prove more misleading than helpful and so those wishing to reach the Way by bus are advised to obtain up-to-date information by phoning the following hotlines:-

Bedfordshire/Luton	: 0345-788788
Buckinghamshire	: 0345-382000
Hertfordshire	: 0345-244344
Oxfordshire	: 01865-810405

While it is hoped that the special maps provided will assist the user to avoid going astray and skeleton details of the surrounding road network are given to enable walkers to vary the route in emergency, it is always advisable to take an Ordnance Survey or Chiltern Society map with you to enable you to vary the route without using roads or get your bearings if you do become seriously lost. Details of the appropriate maps are given in the introductory information for each section.

As for other equipment, readers are advised that some mud will normally be encountered particularly in woodland except in the driest weather. However proper walking boots are to be recommended at all times as, even when there are no mud problems, hard ruts or rough surfaces make the protection given by boots to the ankles desirable. In addition, in some places overgrowth is prevalent around stiles and hedge gaps and in woodland particularly in summer. To avoid resultant discomfort, it is therefore always advisable to carry a stick to clear the way or wear protective clothing.

In order to assist in coordinating the plans and the texts, all the numbers of paths used have been shown on the plans and incorporated into the texts. These numbers, which are also shown on the Chiltern Society's Footpath Maps, consist of the official County Council footpath number with prefix letters used to indicate the parish concerned. It is therefore most helpful to use these when reporting any path problems you may find, together, if possible, with the national grid reference for the precise location of the trouble spot, as, in this way, the problem can be identified on the ground with a minimum of time loss in looking for it. National grid references can, however, only be calculated with the help of Ordnance Survey Landranger, Explorer, Outdoor Leisure or Pathfinder maps and an explanation of how this is done can be found in the Key to all except Pathfinder maps.

The length of time required for any particular section of the Way depends on a number of factors such as your personal walking speed, the number of hills, stiles, etc. to be negotiated, whether or not you stop to rest, eat or drink, investigate places of interest etc. and the number of impediments such as mud, crops, overgrowth, ploughing, etc. which you encounter, but generally an average speed of between two and two and a half miles per hour is about right. It is, however, always advisable to allow extra time if you are limited by the daylight or catching a particular bus or train home in order to avoid your walk developing into a race against the clock.

Should you have problems with any of the paths used or find that the description given is no longer correct, the author would be most grateful if you could let him have details (c/o The Book Castle or the Chiltern Society), so that attempts can be made to rectify the problem or the text can be corrected at the next reprint. Nevertheless, the author hopes that you will not encounter any serious problems and have pleasure from following the Way.

CHILTERN WAY &
Linking Long-Distance Paths

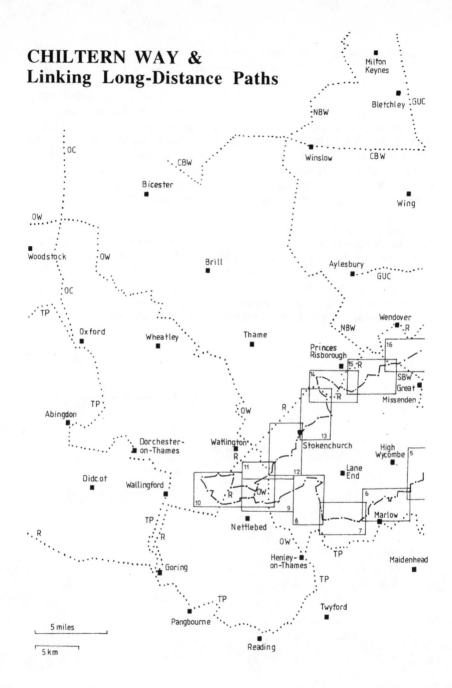

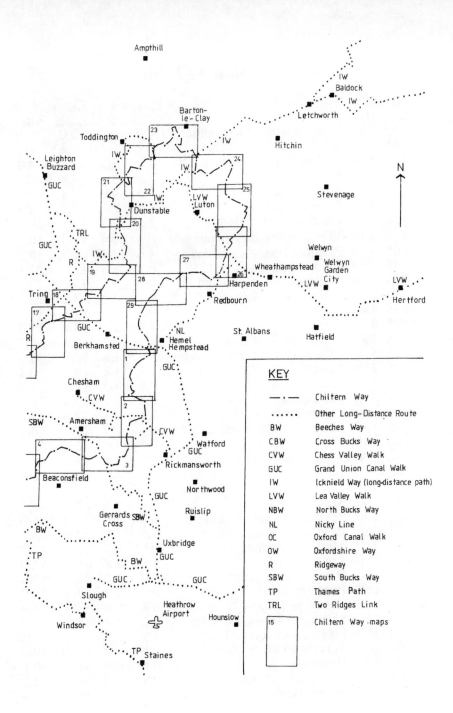

Ampthill

IW
Baldock
IW
Letchworth

Barton-
le-Clay
23
Toddington
IW
Hitchin
IW
24
Leighton
Buzzard
IW
GUC
21
25
Stevenage
22
IW
LVW
20
Luton
Dunstable

TRL
Welwyn
GUC
Welwyn
R
27
Garden
IW
Wheathampstead
City
LVW
19
26
LVW
28
Harpenden
Tring 18
Redbourn
Hertford
17
29
St. Albans
R
GUC
Hatfield
NL
Berkhamsted
Hemel
Hempstead
1
GUC

Chesham
CVW
2
SBW
Amersham
CVW
Watford
4
GUC
Rickmansworth
3
Beaconsfield
Northwood
GUC
Ruislip
Gerrards SBW
Cross
BW
Uxbridge
TP
BW
GUC
GUC
GUC
Slough
Heathrow
Airport
Hounslow
Windsor
TP
Staines

KEY

—·—	Chiltern Way
......	Other Long-Distance Route
BW	Beeches Way
CBW	Cross Bucks Way
CVW	Chess Valley Walk
GUC	Grand Union Canal Walk
IW	Icknield Way (long-distance path)
LVW	Lea Valley Walk
NBW	North Bucks Way
NL	Nicky Line
OC	Oxford Canal Walk
OW	Oxfordshire Way
R	Ridgeway
SBW	South Bucks Way
TP	Thames Path
TRL	Two Ridges Link
15	Chiltern Way maps

Distance Table

Height (m.)	(ft.)	Place	Distance miles	km	Cumulative miles	km
85	280	Hemel Hempstead Station	0.0	0.0	0.0	0.0
85	280	A4251 (A41 Flyover)	0.2	0.3	0.2	0.3
155	510	Bovingdon (Chipperfield Rd)	2.4	3.9	2.6	4.2
135	440	Flaunden	2.0	3.3	4.6	7.5
115	380	Sarratt Church	2.5	4.0	7.1	11.5
125	410	Chenies (A404)	1.5	2.4	8.6	13.9
110	360	Chorleywood West	1.3	2.1	9.9	16.0
120	390	Chorleywood (Heronsgate Rd)	0.4	0.6	10.3	16.6
105	340	Chalfont Park (Gorelands La)	1.6	2.5	11.9	19.1
75	250	Chalfont St. Giles (A413)	0.8	1.3	12.7	20.4
70	230	Chalfont St. Giles (High St)	0.3	0.5	13.0	20.9
80	260	South Bucks Way (CG29/30)	0.8	1.3	13.8	22.2
135	440	Bottrells Lane	0.8	1.3	14.6	23.5
125	410	A355	1.4	2.2	16.0	25.7
165	540	Coleshill ('Red Lion')	0.6	1.0	16.6	26.7
155	510	Winchmore Hill Crossroads	1.0	1.6	17.6	28.3
110	360	Penn Bottom (Car Park)	1.1	1.8	18.7	30.1
165	540	Penn (B474)	0.8	1.3	19.5	31.4
170	560	Penn (Beacon Hill)	0.4	0.7	19.9	32.1
55	180	Loudwater (A40)	2.1	3.3	22.0	35.4
55	180	Loudwater (Kingsmead Rd)	0.4	0.7	22.4	36.1
115	380	Flackwell Heath (Heath End Rd)	0.6	1.0	23.0	37.1
60	200	Sheepridge ('Crooked Billet')	0.9	1.4	23.9	38.5
90	300	Burroughs Grove (official)	2.6	4.1	26.5	42.6
		„ „ (short cut)	2.1	3.4		
55	180	Marlow Bottom	0.9	1.5	27.4	44.1
100	330	Seymour Court (B482)	0.5	0.9	27.9	45.0
85	280	Bovingdon Green (Bucks)	1.1	1.8	29.0	46.8
95	310	Marlow Common	0.9	1.4	29.9	48.2
120	390	Rotten Row	1.8	2.8	31.7	51.0
45	150	Hambleden Church	1.0	1.7	32.7	52.7
50	160	Pheasant's Hill	0.6	1.0	33.3	53.7
55	180	Colstrope	0.4	0.7	33.7	54.4
70	230	Skirmett (Shogmoor Lane)	1.2	1.9	34.9	56.3
80	260	Fingest ('Chequers Inn')	1.7	2.6	36.6	58.9
80	260	Turville (Village Green)	0.6	1.0	37.2	59.9
105	340	Dolesden	0.6	0.9	37.8	60.8
195	640	Southend Common	0.9	1.5	38.7	62.3
90	300	Stonor (village)	1.4	2.3	40.1	64.6

Height		Place	Distance		Cumulative	
(m.)	(ft.)		miles	km	miles	km
180	590	Maidensgrove (Ox. Way)	0.9	1.5	41.0	66.1
190	620	Maidensgrove Common	0.4	0.7	41.4	66.8
135	440	Start of Ewelme Loop	1.0	1.5	42.4	68.3
165	540	End of Loop (via short cut)	0.5	0.8	(42.9)	(69.1)
205	670	Park Corner (B481)	1.1	1.7	43.5	70.0
160	520	Ridgeway (N. of Nuffield)	1.4	2.2	44.9	72.2
90	300	Ewelme (Recreation Ground)	3.0	4.8	47.9	77.0
110	360	Icknieldbank Plantation	1.4	2.3	49.3	79.3
190	620	Swyncombe Down (Ridgeway)	1.1	1.7	50.4	81.0
165	540	Swyncombe Church	0.7	1.3	51.1	82.3
220	720	Cookley Green (B481)	1.0	1.6	52.1	83.9
165	540	End of Ewelme Loop	0.7	1.1	52.8	85.0
195	640	Russell's Water Pond	0.3	0.5	53.1	85.5
170	560	Pishill Bottom (B480/Grove Fm)	0.7	1.1	53.8	86.6
180	590	Oxfordshire Way (College Wd)	1.3	2.1	55.1	88.7
165	540	Oxfordshire Way (Fire Wood)	0.3	0.5	55.4	89.2
220	720	Northend Common	0.6	1.0	56.0	90.2
225	740	Ibstone (N. end of village)	1.8	2.9	57.8	93.1
225	740	Stokenchurch (A40)	1.7	2.7	59.5	95.8
150	490	Radnage Church	2.2	3.5	61.7	99.3
210	690	Bledlow Ridge	0.6	1.0	62.3	100.3
215	710	Rout's Green	0.7	1.2	63.0	101.5
185	610	Ridgeway (W. of Wigan's La)	1.2	2.0	64.2	103.5
115	380	Bledlow (W. of Church)	1.0	1.5	65.2	105.0
105	340	Saunderton Church	1.3	2.1	66.5	107.1
125	410	Ridgeway (S. of Saunderton)	0.7	1.1	67.2	108.2
140	460	A4010	0.6	1.0	67.8	109.2
225	740	Lacey Green ('Whip')	0.8	1.2	68.6	110.4
210	690	Lily Bottom	0.9	1.5	69.5	111.9
230	750	Redland End	0.5	0.8	70.0	112.7
215	710	Hampden House	0.9	1.5	70.9	114.2
165	540	Hampden Bottom	0.6	0.9	71.5	115.1
210	690	Little Hampden (S. Bucks Way)	0.9	1.5	72.4	116.6
220	720	Cobblers Hill (S. Bucks Way)	0.7	1.1	73.1	117.7
145	480	Wendover Dean (A413)	0.9	1.5	74.0	119.2
205	670	Lee Gate ('Gate')	1.2	2.0	75.2	121.2
200	660	Kingswood ('Old Swan')	0.4	0.6	75.6	121.8
200	660	St. Leonard's ('White Lion')	1.7	2.7	77.3	124.5
195	640	Wigginton (Chesham Road)	2.6	4.2	79.9	128.7
120	390	Cow Roast (A4251)	1.6	2.5	81.5	131.2
120	390	Cow Roast Lock (GUC)	0.1	0.1	81.6	131.3

Height		Place	Distance		Cumulative	
(m.)	(ft.)		miles	km	miles	km
160	520	Aldbury (Malting Lane)	1.6	2.7	83.2	134.0
190	620	B4506	0.7	1.2	83.9	135.2
190	620	Little Gaddesden (P.H.)	1.6	2.6	85.5	137.8
120	390	A4146	1.3	2.1	86.8	139.9
185	610	Studham (Common Road)	1.0	1.5	87.8	141.4
215	710	Whipsnade (B4540)	2.3	3.7	90.1	145.1
230	750	Dunstable Downs (Car Park)	1.4	2.2	91.5	147.3
165	540	Dunstable (B489/B4541)	1.0	1.6	92.5	148.9
110	360	Sewell (bend in road)	1.4	2.4	93.9	151.3
125	410	A5 ('Chalk Hill')	1.1	1.7	95.0	153.0
115	380	Bidwell (A5120/'Old Red Lion')	1.1	1.7	96.1	154.7
105	340	Chalton (B579/'Star')	2.8	4.6	98.9	159.3
160	520	Upper Sundon ('Red Lion')	1.4	2.3	100.3	161.6
155	510	Sundon Hills Country Park	0.9	1.4	101.2	163.0
150	490	Sharpenhoe Clappers (road)	1.8	2.9	103.0	165.9
125	410	A6 (Barton Hill)	1.7	2.7	104.7	168.6
155	510	Streatley Church	0.6	1.0	105.3	169.6
130	430	A6 (Swedish Cottages)	0.7	1.1	106.0	170.7
150	490	Icknield Way (Maulden Firs)	1.3	2.1	107.3	172.8
185	610	Galley Hill	0.1	0.2	107.4	173.0
195	640	Warden Hill	0.8	1.3	108.2	174.3
180	590	Stopsley (Whitehill Farm)	1.4	2.3	109.6	176.6
140	460	Lilley Church	1.2	1.8	110.8	178.4
135	440	Hollybush Hill (Glebe Farm)	0.9	1.5	111.7	179.9
120	390	Lilley Bottom	0.8	1.3	112.5	181.2
165	540	Mangrove Green	1.1	1.8	113.6	183.0
155	510	Cockernhoe Green	0.3	0.5	113.9	183.5
150	490	Wandon End Farm	1.0	1.5	114.9	185.0
145	480	Breachwood Green	1.2	2.0	116.1	187.0
145	480	Peter's Green	2.1	3.3	118.2	190.3
95	310	East Hyde (B653)	1.6	2.6	119.8	192.9
110	360	Harpenden (A1081)	1.4	2.2	121.2	195.1
110	360	M1 (Junction 9)	3.0	4.8	124.2	199.9
145	480	Flamstead Church	1.0	1.7	125.2	201.6
165	540	Gaddesden Row School	2.4	3.8	127.6	205.4
105	340	Water End (A4146)	1.8	3.0	129.4	208.4
160	520	Potten End (Water End Rd)	1.1	1.7	130.5	210.1
160	520	Fields End	0.9	1.5	131.4	211.6
85	280	Boxmoor (Grand Union Canal)	1.6	2.5	133.0	214.1
85	280	A4251 (A41 Flyover)	0.2	0.3	133.2	214.4
85	280	Hemel Hempstead Station	0.2	0.3	133.4	214.7

GUIDE TO THE CHILTERN WAY

Hemel Hempstead Station - Bovingdon (Herts.) (Map 1)

Maps
OS Landranger Sheet 166
OS Explorer Sheet 182
OS Pathfinder Sheet 1119 (TL00/10)
Chiltern Society FP Maps Nos. 5 & 20

Parking
Hemel Hempstead Station car park.

To unfamiliar readers, Hemel Hempstead Station may seem an unlikely starting point for the Chiltern Way, as the town as a post-war ´new town` may conjure up visions of endless housing estates rather than beechwoods and bluebells, but its location is hilly so that it is surrounded by good walking country and ´green lungs` have been left between the estates so that parts of the town can be traversed by walkers with only a minimum of intrusion by urban development. In fact, as the Way was conceived as a continuous circular route and a starting point was only needed for the purposes of this guide, the reason for its choice was that it happened to be the point on the existing proposed route with the best public transport access being only 300 yards from the circular route.

Despite the post-war ´new town` designation Hemel Hempstead in fact has a long history as the A4251, on which the station is situated, is part of a Roman road known as Akeman Street and remains of Roman villas have been found not only here but also in Gadebridge Park to the north of the town centre. In the Middle Ages Hemel Hempstead must already have been a wealthy market town as is attested by its magnificent twelfth-century church and in the eighteenth and nineteenth centuries the construction of the Grand Junction Canal, the L&NWR main line from London (Euston) to the Midlands and North and several paper mills where modern paper-making methods were pioneered, all to the south of the mediæval town, caused its expansion southwards and the absorption of neighbouring villages such as Boxmoor where the railway station is situated.

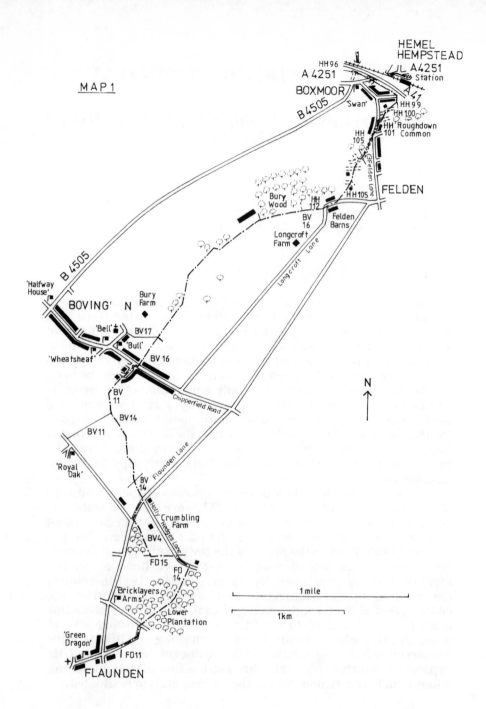

MAP 1

HEMEL HEMPSTEAD

HH96
A 4251
BOXMOOR
B4505
A4251
Station

'Swan'
HH99
HH 100
HH 'Roughdown
101 Common
HH 105
Felden Lane
FELDEN
HH 105
HH 112
Bury Wood
BV 16
Felden Barns
Longcroft Farm
Longcroft Lane
B 4505
'Halfway House'
BOVING' N
Bury Farm
'Bell'
BV17
'Bull'
BV 16
'Wheatsheaf'
BV 11
Chipperfield Road
N
BV14
BV 11
Flaunden Lane
'Royal Oak'
BV 14
Holly Hedges Lane
Crumbling Farm
BV4
FD15
FD 14
'Bricklayers Arms'
Lower Plantation
'Green Dragon'
FD11
FLAUNDEN

1 mile

1 km

16

Starting from the main entrance to Hemel Hempstead Station, turn left down the station approach to reach a roundabout. Here cross the A4251 left of the roundabout and turn left onto its footway passing under three bridges carrying the railway and the A41.

Now recross the main road and, **joining the main route of the Chiltern Way**, take fenced path HH99 off the end of a short cul-de-sac. On reaching the entrance to a subway to your left, bear half right, ignoring a gravel lane to your right and passing through a kissing-gate frame, then take an enclosed path uphill to a kissing-gate into woodland on Roughdown Common. Here fork right onto path HH100 climbing gently through the wood and soon passing between bollards to join a flinty drive. Soon after the drive bears right, fork left onto a woodland path climbing gently to reach another flinty track (byway HH101) then turn right onto this, soon reaching Felden Lane.

Turn left onto this road, then, just past its junction with Roefields Close, fork right onto path HH105 following the macadam drive to Felden Lodge through woodland onto a golf course. By a single ash tree to your right, leave the drive and bear half left across a fairway to a kissing-gate in the top hedge. Here cross a bridleway and go through a kissing-gate opposite then bear slightly right across a meadow, passing the corner of a garden hedge to your right to reach a kissing-gate by a garage. Now cross a cottage drive and follow a left-hand hedge straight on to a stile, then follow a right-hand hedge straight on across a field to a squeeze-stile leading to Longcroft Lane.

Turn right onto this road passing Felden Barns, then at a left-hand bend fork right over a stile onto path HH112 following what is normally a crop-break straight on across a field (soon on path BV16) to reach a gap in the next hedge. Now bear slightly right across the next field to join the edge of Bury Wood to your right level with a large clump of bushes to your left concealing a pond. Here ignore a branching path into the wood and follow its outside edge, disregarding all further paths into the wood then continuing beside a right-hand hedge to the far end of the field. Now cross a stile and, ignoring a gate to your right, bear slightly left and follow a fenced path past a copse to cross another stile, then turn right and follow the right-hand hedge to a field corner. Here turn left and continue beside the right-hand hedge for over half a mile to cross a stile at the far end of the field. Now with views to your right of Bovingdon Church and still on path BV16, follow a left-hand hedge straight on to cross a stile into a path between gardens which eventually leads you out to Chipperfield Road in Bovingdon, onto which you turn right.

17

Bovingdon (Herts.) - Flaunden (Map 1)

Maps
OS Landranger Sheet 166
OS Explorer Sheet 182
OS Pathfinder Sheet 1119 (TL00/10)
Chiltern Society FP Map No.5

Parking
On-street parking is possible in Bovingdon.

**Much of Bovingdon today with its housing estates, ´infill´ develop-
ment, shops etc. has a very suburban appearance, but quiet
corners remain and the village can boast a number of attractive
houses and cottages, some of which date back to the sixteenth or
seventeenth century. The picturesque well in the village centre
was built in 1881 in memory of a Lord of the Manor, Granville
Dudley Ryder from a nearby manor house known as Westbrook
Hay who died in 1879, while the church, set in one of the largest
churchyards in Hertfordshire, was rebuilt in 1845 on the site of a
thirteenth-century predecessor, from which part of the tower and
the effigy of a knight dating from around 1400 are preserved.
Until 1833 the then small village of Bovingdon was merely a
hamlet of Hemel Hempstead and it is said that services were only
held in the ruinous old church once a month if bad weather did
not discourage the curate from coming from Hemel to take them!**

After 30 yards by a footpath sign to your left, turn left across the
grass verge and take a road called Austins Mead straight on. Where
the road turns right, just past a small car park on your left, fork left
onto path BV11, an alleyway between houses nos. 51 and 52
leading to a stile. Now follow a right-hand hedge straight on to a
second stile, then bear half left across a field to a stile in the far
corner. Here take path BV14 bearing half left across the next field
to cross a stile at a corner of a hedge hidden by a holly tree, then
follow a left-hand hedge straight on. Where the hedge turns left,
leave it and bear half right across the field to a corner of another
hedge, then bear half left and follow this hedge to the stile of a
crossing path to your right. Here bear slightly left and follow a
right-hand fence, later a hedge to cross a stile by a gate leading to a
road junction.

Turn right onto the priority road (Flaunden Lane), then, just
before another road junction, turn left over a stile and take path

BV4 following the edge of a wood through two fields. On passing through a hedge gap into a third field, turn left onto path FD15 following a left-hand line of trees to cross a stile in a field corner, then go straight on across the next field, passing right of two oak trees to reach a kissing-gate by iron gates into Holly Hedges Lane onto which you turn right. After 170 yards where woodland commences to your right, turn right over a stile by a disused gate onto path FD14 following the edge of the wood to the far side of a right-hand field, then keeping straight on through the wood to a road junction. Here cross the priority road and take the Flaunden road straight on gently uphill to reach the Flaunden village nameboard.

Flaunden - Sarratt Church (Map 2)

Maps
OS Landranger Sheet 166
OS Explorer Sheets 172 & 182
OS Pathfinder Sheets 1119 (TL00/10) & 1139 (TQ09/19)
Chiltern Society FP Map No.5

Parking
Limited on-street parking in Flaunden village. Take care not to obstruct or park opposite driveways in the narrow village streets.

Flaunden, locally pronounced 'Flarnden', is an unspoilt secluded village clustered around a crossroads of narrow lanes on a hill-top north of the Chess valley. The village church, built in 1838 to replace a thirteenth-century predecessor over a mile away in the Chess valley, is notable for being the first to be designed by the celebrated architect, Sir George Gilbert Scott, who was later responsible for the Midland Grand Hotel in London which forms the façade of St. Pancras Station. This church incorporates several items from its predecessor including its fifteenth-century font, three ancient bells and the one-handed church clock.

Just past the Flaunden village nameboard where the road widens, turn left over a stile by a gate onto path FD11 following a right-hand hedge gently uphill to cross a stile. Now bear half left across the next field heading for a gap between trees to cross another stile and take a fenced path beside a left-hand hedge to reach a narrow lane. Turn right onto this road passing Newhouse Farm then turn left through a hedge gap onto path SA51 following a left-hand hedge at first. Where the hedge turns left, bear slightly right across the field to a stile and steps leading down into a narrow lane. Turn left onto this road then, after some 350 yards at the entrance to Great Bragman's Farm, fork right over a stile onto path SA25 bearing slightly right across a field to cross a concealed stile at the far end of a weatherboarded barn where the timber-framed farmhouse can be seen to your right. Now follow a hedged path straight on, crossing another stile and continuing to Rosehall Farm.

By an entrance to the farm bear slightly right along the concrete road, bearing slightly left at one fork and slightly right at a second and continuing along a rough road, soon passing Rosehall Wood to your left and a belt of trees to your right. Now ignore a gate to your right and where the farm road turns left, leave it, crossing a stile by a gate under an oak tree and taking path SA24 beside a right-hand fence to a stile in a field corner. Having crossed this, bear slightly right across the next field to cross two stiles by gates in the far corner. Here bear half right across the next field aiming for a junction of hedges to cross a stile leading into Moor Lane, then cross a stile opposite and follow a left-hand hedge to a further stile. Now bear half right across the next field to a stile into the corner of a wood where you take the obvious path beside a row of cypress trees to your right to reach a kissing-gate. Here disregard a branching path to your right, then at a crossways turn right onto a gravelly track and follow it through woodland on Dawes Common, ignoring all branching and crossing paths, to reach Dawes Lane.

Cross this narrow road and take path SA24 through a kissing-gate by a disused gate opposite, soon passing between fenced plantations. Now ignore a branching path to your left and continue, passing through another kissing-gate and following a right-hand fence to a kissing-gate onto a rough road. Take this straight on, ignoring a branching drive to your right and paths to your left. At a left-hand bend fork right through a kissing-gate and over a stile. Now follow a left-hand fence along the outside edge of a wood with views of the Chess valley to your right, then, where the fence turns left, leave it and go straight on, heading just right of Sarratt church tower to reach a stile and kissing-gate into the churchyard.

Sarratt Church - Chenies (Map 2)

Maps
OS Landranger Sheets 166 or 176
OS Explorer Sheet 172
OS Pathfinder Sheet 1139 (TQ09/19)
Chiltern Society FP Map No.5

Parking
On-street parking is possible at Sarratt Green two-thirds of a mile north of the church. Do not use the ´Cock Inn` car park without the landlord´s permission.

Sarratt Church, situated in the old village known as Church End, is a cruciform twelfth-century building appropriately dedicated to the Holy Cross. It is of particular interest as its tower was rebuilt in the fifteenth century in part with Roman bricks (presumably from the ruins of a Roman villa discovered in the vicinity) and it is also the only church tower in Hertfordshire with a saddleback roof. The church, restored by Sir George Gilbert Scott in 1865, also contains a Norman font, a fragment of a thirteenth-century wall painting and a carved Jacobean pulpit, from which the renowned Nonconformist Richard Baxter preached in the seventeenth century. Also at Church End are a pub, a nineteenth-century manor house and some almshouses rebuilt in 1821, but the bulk of the modern village is situated around Sarratt´s extensive village green two-thirds of a mile to the north.

If wishing to visit the church or the ´Cock Inn`, take path SA53 straight on into the churchyard then, for the pub, bear half left, passing left of the church to reach the lychgate leading to Church Lane where the ´Cock Inn` is to your left.

Otherwise, do **not** enter the churchyard but turn sharp right onto path SA39 following a left-hand hedge to a gate and stile into a tree belt. Cross this stile then turn left onto path SA32 following a left-hand hedge downhill with superb views to your right up the Chess valley. In the bottom corner of the field cross a stile, descend some steps and follow a fenced path downhill to a path junction by a kissing-gate. Go through the kissing-gate and now in Bucks, turn right onto path CN15 following a right-hand fence to cross a stile and a footbridge over the River Chess. Here go straight on through marshland to cross another footbridge. Now, at a three-way fork, take the central option straight on, passing left of a large elderbush, ignoring a crossing path and crossing a stile into Turvey Lane Wood. Go straight on through this wood disregarding the stile of a branching path to your right and continuing along a track up a valley bottom for over a third of a mile, eventually emerging through a gap by an overgrown stile into a field. Here bear half left uphill to the right-hand corner of Wyburn Wood. Now cross a stile into this wood and go straight on through it to a stile into the corner of a field, then follow a right-hand hedge straight on to a stile into a fenced path leading to a gate onto a road in Chenies.

Chenies - Chorleywood West (Map 2)

Maps
OS Landranger Sheets 166 or 176
OS Explorer Sheet 172
OS Pathfinder Sheet 1139 (TQ09/19)
Chiltern Society FP Map No.5

Parking
There are laybys near Chenies on the A404 and on-street parking is possible in the village.

Chenies, which belonged to the Earls and Dukes of Bedford and their predecessors by marriage, the Cheyne family, from the thirteenth century till 1954, is today a picturesque model village largely rebuilt by the Estate in the nineteenth century. Its fine Manor, once known as Chenies Palace as both Henry VIII and Elizabeth I stayed there, is in part fifteenth-century but mainly dates from 1530 when it was extended by the 1st Earl of Bedford while the fifteenth-century church is noted for the Bedford Chapel with its superb monuments dating from 1556. Originally known as Isenhampstead, the village name evolved in the thirteenth century to Isenhampstead Cheynes and only contracted to its present form in the nineteenth century.

Now cross the village street and turn right onto its footway passing the Old Rectory. After 100 yards, where the village inns are straight ahead, turn left through a kissing-gate onto path CN25. Now follow a right-hand hedge across the cricket field then pass through a kissing-gate and continue beside the right-hand hedge. Where the hedge bears right, leave it and go straight on across the field to another kissing-gate then continue between a hedge and a fence to a stile onto a road where the Manor is to your right. Turn left onto this road to reach the A404, then cross this main road carefully and take bridleway CN3 straight on, entering a sunken green lane and following it gently downhill for half a mile, passing through Halsey´s Wood and reaching a tunnel under the Metropolitan Line built in 1889 and now jointly used by Chiltern Railways.

At the far end of the tunnel go past a gate into Whitelands Wood reentering Hertfordshire. Now ignoring a branching path to your left, take bridleway CW-CN3 straight on along a woodland track beside a right-hand hedge disregarding branching paths to your left. Where the hedge bears away to the right, take the track straight on downhill and up again ignoring all branching or crossing paths or tracks to reach a gate at the edge of the wood. Here disregard a crossing path and a path forking right through a squeeze-stile into a plantation and walk round the right-hand end of a gate then take a fenced track along the outside edge of Hillas Wood with Chorleywood West coming into view ahead, later leaving the wood behind and taking a fenced track straight on, passing Newhouse Farm with its tall cedar to your right. On reaching its drive (bridleway CN3a), turn left onto it (briefly reentering Bucks) and follow it to a road junction in Chorleywood West.

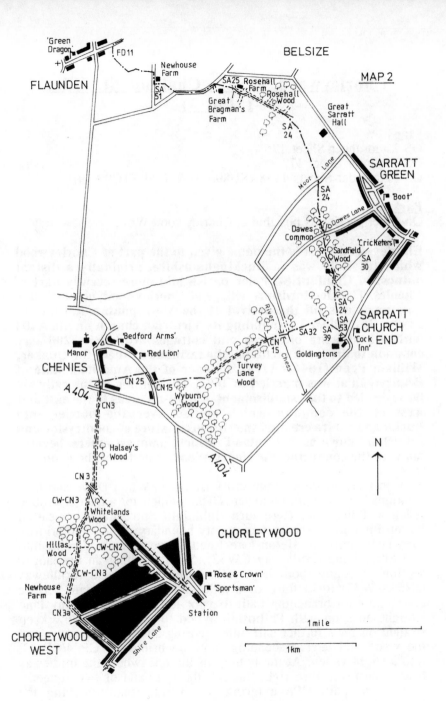

Chorleywood West - Chalfont St. Giles (Map 3)

Maps
OS Landranger Sheet 176
OS Explorer Sheet 172
OS Pathfinder Sheets 1138 (SU89/99) & 1139 (TQ09/19)

Parking
On-street parking is possible at Chorleywood West.

Chorleywood West is the name given to the part of Chorleywood which till 1992 was in Buckinghamshire, originally a distant outpost of Chalfont St. Peter parish and more recently part of Chenies. The Hertfordshire village of Chorleywood, of which it is now part, was till the arrival of the Metropolitan Railway in 1889 a tiny village surrounding its Victorian church on the A404 with a scattering of farms and cottages around its 200-acre common to the south including the farmhouse where the Quaker, William Penn (1644 - 1718), founder of the American state of Pennsylvania, was married in 1672. The coming of the railway, however, led to the establishment of built-up areas to the east and west of the common which spilled over the border into Buckinghamshire creating the curious mixture of countryside and suburbia known as ´Metroland`, which, amongst others, became home to the conductor, Sir Henry Wood, founder of the Proms.

Now in Hertfordshire again, cross Blacketts Wood Drive and take Chalfont Lane straight on towards The Swillett for a quarter mile to reach a T-junction. Here turn right into Shire Lane, so called because it follows the ancient county boundary. Where the priority road bears left into Heronsgate Road, leave it, forking right into Old Shire Lane (bridleway CW33). Soon reaching an unchanged section of county boundary, follow this access road (bridleway CN52/CW33) for a third of a mile. Where its macadam surface ends, ignore a branching path to your left and take a stony lane straight on soon with Philipshill Wood to your right. Now keep straight on for a further half mile ignoring all branching paths into the wood and later descending (now on bridleway CP44/CW33) into a slight valley. At the bottom of the hill, where the bridleway bears sharp left, turn right through the left-hand of two squeeze-stiles onto path CP6 entering the wood, finally leaving the Hertfordshire boundary behind and following a chestnut paling fence. After 300 yards you bear left and climb, now with a barbed-wire fence to your right which you follow when the chestnut paling fence ends, eventually crossing a stile into Newland Park where the Chiltern Open Air Museum can be seen to your left.

The Open Air Museum, which can be reached by turning left onto the Newland Park drive 700 yards ahead, was conceived by the Chiltern Society as a project for European Architectural Heritage Year 1975 and was founded on County Council-owned land in Newland Park the following year. Opened to the public in 1981, the constantly-expanding museum consists largely of buildings of architectural interest which would otherwise have been lost through demolition but have instead been painstakingly taken down and rebuilt at Newland Park. It is open daily from April to October from 10 a.m. to 5 p.m.

Follow the right-hand hedge then the edge of Shrubs Wood straight on through the park. At the far side of the wood bear slightly right across a field to cross a stile by a chestnut tree left of a lodge. Now turn right onto the Newland Park drive and follow it to its T-junction with Gorelands Lane. Bear slightly right across this road and take bridleway CP8 through a gap by an overgrown gate opposite, then continue for a third of a mile through a strip of woodland to reach a gap by a gate into Chesham Lane. Cross this road and before crossing the stile opposite, take a few steps to your left for a view of Ashwell's Farm with its fine seventeenth-century timber-framed brick farmhouse and weatherboarded barn.

Now cross the stile and take fenced path CP9 beside a left-hand hedge. On reaching two stiles, cross both, ignoring a branching path to your right, then bear slightly right across a field to cross a stile in the next hedge. Now keep straight on across the next field to a stile in its far corner, then continue along a fenced path to a path junction. Here bear right onto fenced path CG32 and follow it gently downhill for 350 yards to reach the A413 at Chalfont St. Giles. Cross this main road carefully and take the continuation of path CG32 down an alleyway opposite to a kissing-gate into the Misbourne meadows where a fine view of St. Giles's Church opens out ahead. Now bear slightly right, passing through another kissing-gate then ignoring a stile to your right and continuing beside a right-hand fence to a kissing-gate and footbridge over the River Misbourne. Joining the South Bucks Way, disregard a stile to your left, then bear right then left and take a fenced macadam path along the edge of the churchyard, eventually reaching an archway leading into the High Street opposite the 'Crown'.

Chalfont St. Giles - Bottom House Farm Lane (Map 3)

Maps
OS Landranger Sheets 175 or 176
OS Explorer Sheet 172 (or old Sheet 3)
OS Pathfinder Sheet 1138 (SU89/99)
Chiltern Society FP Map No.6

Parking
Signposted car park in Chalfont St. Giles village.

Chalfont St. Giles, despite considerable modern expansion, can still boast a picturesque village centre with its small village green surrounded by attractive little shops, cottages and inns. The church, which is of twelfth-century origin but was remodelled in the fifteenth century and is linked to the green by an archway beneath part of a sixteenth-century cottage, is famous for its mediæval wall paintings and is where the circus proprietor Bertram Mills is buried. The most notable building in the village, however, is Milton´s Cottage, where the poet took refuge from the plague in 1665. Built in about 1600, this cottage was where John Milton completed his ´Paradise Lost ` and it was while he was staying here that Thomas Ellwood, who had secured it for Milton, is said to have inspired Milton to write his ´Paradise Regained `.

Cross the High Street and turn right crossing the entrance to a road called Up Corner, then turn left onto path CG30 following a stony private road called Stratton Chase Drive, soon passing along an avenue of fine chestnut and lime trees. At a left-hand bend fork right off the private road, soon joining a right-hand fence, leaving the trees and continuing between fences to some bungalows where the path becomes a rough road and continues to a bend in Mill Lane where the timber-framed Chalfont Mill to your right, reputed to be the oldest watermill in the county, is well worth a detour.

Now go straight on along Mill Lane, then, at a left-hand bend, leave it and take path CG30 straight on along a fenced track. Where the track ends, ignore a gate to your right and take a narrow path straight on through scrubland into Bycroft Plantation. Here continue within the right-hand edge of this wood ignoring branching paths to your left. Having passed the stile of a branching path in the right-hand fence, continue for a further 230 yards, then, just past a gap to your right by the corner of a field, leaving the South

28

MAP 3

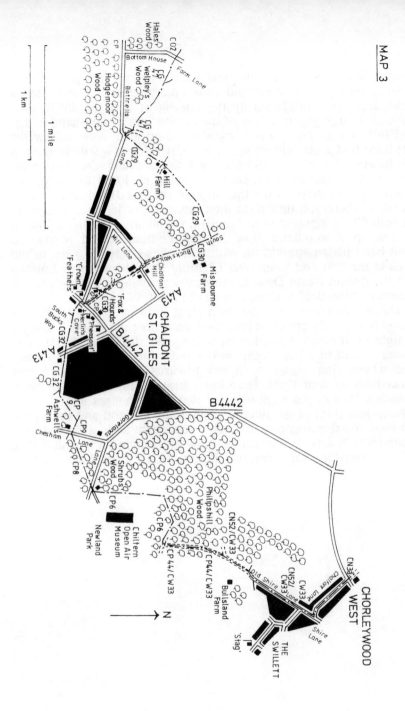

Bucks Way, turn left onto waymarked branching path CG29 passing through the wood and soon emerging over a stile into a field. Here go straight on up the bottom of a slight dip to pass through a large gap in a line of trees, then join a right-hand hedge and follow it to cross a stile by a wired-up gate. Now follow the left-hand hedge straight on uphill for 350 yards to a stile in the top left-hand corner of the field leading into scrubland. Go straight on through this with the path soon becoming enclosed by hedges to reach a gravel drive. Take this straight on past Hill Farm to a T-junction where you turn right then immediately left into scrubland on path CG29 signposted to Froghall, eventually crossing a stile in an outcrop of woodland. Now, leaving the trees behind, follow the right-hand hedge straight on with wide views through gaps in the trees to the east and south over Chalfont St. Giles towards London and the distant North Downs, eventually reaching a kissing-gate in a corner of the field leading to a bend in Bottrells Lane.

Do not join this road, but turn right onto path CG47 taking a gravel lane gently uphill. Where the lane bears right, leave it and go straight on through a gap left of some gates then bear slightly left across a field to a hedge gap with a redundant stile left of an ash tree where fine views open out towards Coleshill ahead and Amersham to your right. Here keep straight on, heading towards Coleshill House, the right-hand of two white houses at Coleshill, passing just right of an outcrop of Welpley´s Wood and through a dip then crossing one rise to reach a redundant stile at the top of a second which acts as a waymark. Now go straight on downhill to a stile and steps leading down into Bottom House Farm Lane.

Bottom House Farm Lane - Coleshill (Map 4)

Maps
OS Landranger Sheets 165 & 175 or 176
OS Explorer Sheet 172 (or old Sheet 3)
OS Pathfinder Sheet 1138 (SU89/99)
Chiltern Society FP Map No.6

Parking
Picnic area and car parks in Bottrells Lane with access to or from
the Chiltern Way via Bottom House Farm Lane, path CO3 (at
Brentford Grange Farm) or the A355.

Cross Bottom House Farm Lane and take path CO2 straight on over
a stile opposite following a left-hand hedge over a rise, then crossing a stile into a second field and continuing beside the left-hand
hedge until you reach a stile in it. Cross this and follow the other
side of the hedge straight on through two fields. In the second field
where the hedge bears right, leave it and go straight on across the
field to cross a stile under an oak tree in the next hedge then follow
a right-hand hedge straight on to a stile onto the drive of a weatherboarded cottage. Here go straight on over another stile opposite
and across a field passing Brentford Grange Farm to your right to
cross a stile under a small oak tree in the next hedge. Now continue
through a plantation, ignoring branching path CO3 to your left and
joining a right-hand fence. Just past a gateway in this fence turn
right over a stile then turn left and follow a left-hand hedge for
over a quarter mile to the A355.
　　Cross this road carefully bearing slightly left and taking the
continuation of path CO2 down a steep flight of steps to cross a
footbridge. Now go straight on through a hedge gap, then keep
right of a hedge and follow it straight on for a third of a mile with
views of the eighteenth-century Coleshill House on the ridge to
your right in places, ignoring a crossing path and eventually reaching the edge of Herts Wood. Here turn right and follow its outside
edge, gradually bearing left to reach a field corner where you take
a shady green lane straight on, eventually emerging at the side of
the ´Red Lion` in Coleshill and continuing through its car park to
the village street near the church and duckpond.

Coleshill - Winchmore Hill (Map 4)

Maps

OS Landranger Sheet 165
OS Explorer Sheet 172 (or old Sheet 3)
OS Pathfinder Sheet 1138 (SU89/99)
Chiltern Society FP Map No.6

Parking

On-street parking is possible in Coleshill village and there is a picnic area in Whielden Lane with access to or from the Chiltern Way via path P83.

Coleshill, on its high ridge above Amersham, was till 1832 a detached enclave of Hertfordshire surrounded by Bucks. As such, in the seventeenth century it afforded a refuge to local Quakers persecuted by the authorities as they were safe here from the Buckinghamshire magistrates and when their Hertfordshire colleagues did make the long trip to Coleshill, the Quakers could quickly flee across the border into Bucks. One notable Quaker to live in Coleshill at this time was Thomas Ellwood, a friend of the poet John Milton, who lived for many years at Hunger Hill Farm (now Ongar Hill Farm) to the south of the village, but the farm you see today is not that of Thomas Ellwood as it was rebuilt in 1873. This is, however, not the village´s only literary association as Coleshill, which, with its windmill, common and attractive duckpond, remains a rural oasis within 25 miles of Central London, was in 1606 the birthplace of the poet Edmund Waller, whose sixteenth-century home known as Stock Place still stands in the centre of the village near the ´Red Lion` and Victorian church, designed by George Street in 1861.

Now cross the village street and take path CO6 straight on between safety barriers and along a hedged macadam path, passing the church to your right to reach Manor Way. Bear slightly left across this road and take the continuation of path CO6 along the gravel drive to Lands Farm. Where the drive forks at the farm entrance, keep right, then ignore branching drives to your right to reach a gate and stile. Cross the stile and take a concrete road straight on, continuing along a wide fenced grassy track by a left-hand hedge to a gate. Here fork left onto path CO7 crossing a stile left of the gate and taking a fenced path beside the left-hand hedge to reach a stile into the next field. Now turn left and follow a left-hand fence to a corner then bear half right across the field to pass the left-hand end of a small copse where you bear slightly right down the field to reach a hedge gap in the bottom corner into West Wood. Here take a woodland track straight on, ignoring branching tracks and paths to left and right. On emerging into another field, take path P82, keeping right of a hedge ahead and following it straight on through two fields with fine views towards Winchmore Hill ahead and across the woods to your right, above which rises the spire of Penn Street Church built by the first Earl Howe in 1849. At the far side of the second field go straight on into an old green lane which leads you to a village street in Winchmore Hill called The Hill opposite the Methodist Church, onto which you turn left.

Winchmore Hill - Penn (Map 4)

Maps
OS Landranger Sheet 175
OS Explorer Sheet 172 (or old Sheet 3)
OS Pathfinder Sheet 1138 (SU89/99)
Chiltern Society FP Map No.6

Parking
On-street parking is possible in Winchmore Hill village and there is a small parking area in Crown Lane, Penn Bottom near the entrance to path P25.

Winchmore Hill, with its large green by a crossroads with two pubs and one (formerly two) Methodist chapels, though no parish church, may seem the epitome of a Bucks Chiltern village. It is now a hamlet of Penn parish, but till 1955 it was largely in Coleshill (and consequently till 1832 in Hertfordshire) with smaller parts in Amersham and Penn. The fact that the three parishes and two counties met at its crossroads also gave rise to its name deriving from the Old English ´wincel` (meaning angle) and ´mær` (meaning boundary) thus combining as ´angled boundary hill`.

Now go gently up The Hill to a crossroads by the ´Plough Inn`. Here cross the priority road and turn right onto path P8 across the green, heading for a tall holly tree at the right-hand end of a garden hedge protruding onto the green, then continuing past it to reach a hedge gap leading to a stile. Having crossed this stile, take a raised path straight on across a field to cross a stile by gates leading to Horsemoor Lane near a very old pond called Gardswater. Cross this road and a stile by a gate opposite, then ignore the stile of a branching path ahead and take path P11 bearing left into a strip of woodland. Follow this obvious path straight on through the strip of woodland for nearly a quarter mile, eventually ignoring a branching path to your left and reaching a macadam drive to Penn House. This mile-long banked track was built in the 1930s by the fifth Earl Howe to practise racing his fleet of cars. Bear left onto this and follow it for 250 yards, then at a left-hand bend fork right onto a track following the edge of Branches Wood, soon joining another track which merges from your left and leaving the wood. Here bear slightly left, following a grassy track beside a right-hand hedge downhill passing Round Wood to your right then bearing right to reach a road in Penn Bottom.

Turn right onto this road, then at a right-hand bend fork left into Crown Lane passing a copse to your right and reaching Church Knoll with its sarsen stones and small car park. The knoll to your right, on which a house now stands, is thought to be the site of a Saxon church, which would have been more central to Penn parish than the present fourteenth-century building on the ridge to the south.

Now turn right onto path P25 following a gravel track. At a fork take a path between hedges just right of the left-hand option straight on. On entering a field, follow its left-hand hedge straight on, soon joining a grassy track, then ignore a crossing path and continue beside a left-hand hedge to the far end of the field. Now on path P71, go straight on through a hedge gap and follow a grassy track beside a left-hand hedge straight on to a corner of Twichels Wood. About 30 yards further on, turn left over a concealed stile into the wood, then bear right and follow an obvious, if sometimes overgrown, path through the wood, eventually emerging over a stile onto a grassy track. Here bear half left across the corner of a field aiming for the right-hand end of a large clump of trees, then continue past this clump and the left-hand side of a second clump to reach the back of a roadside hedge. Now bear right to cross a stile onto the B474 at Penn and turn sharp left onto its footway.

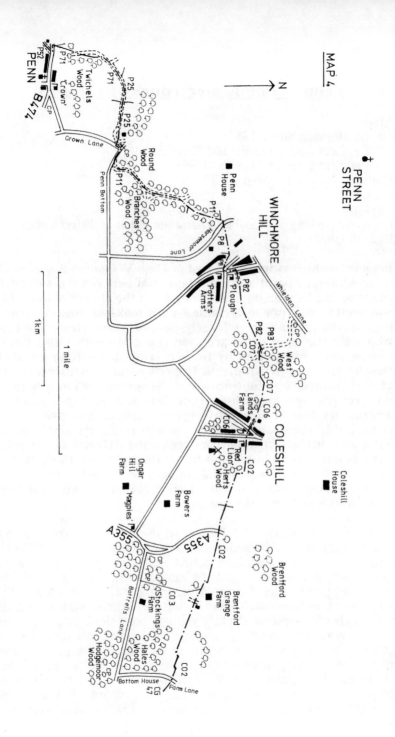

MAP 4

N

PENN STREET

PENN

B474

P52
P71
P71
P71
Twitchels Wood
'Crown'
CP
P25
P25
P25
Crown Lane
Round Wood
CP
Penn House
P11
Penn Bottom
Branches Wood
P11
Horsemoor Lane
WINCHMORE HILL
P8
P8
P8
P8
'Potters Arms'
'Plough'
P82
P82
P82
Whielden Lane
CP
P83
C07
C07
West Wood
C07
C07
C06
Lands Farm
C06
C06
COLESHILL
C02
'Red Lion'
X
Herts Wood
Ongar Hill Farm
'Magpies'
Bowers Farm
A355
A355
C02
Coleshill House
Brentford Wood
Brentford Grange Farm
CP
C03
4Stockings Farm
Hales Wood
C02
CP
Barrells Lane
Hodgemoor Wood
Bottom House
Farm Lane
CG 47
C02

1km

1 mile

35

Penn - Loudwater (Bucks.) (Map 5)

Maps
OS Landranger Sheet 175
OS Explorer Sheet 172 (or old Sheet 3)
OS Pathfinder Sheet 1138 (SU89/99)
Chiltern Society FP Map No.13

Parking
On-street parking is possible around the green at Tylers Green or at Beacon Hill.

Penn on its high ridge to the east of High Wycombe is potentially quite a vantage point as locals claim that between ten and twelve counties can be seen on a clear day from the church tower which was used in wartime as a Home Guard look-out post. At ground level buildings and trees largely conceal these views but those who walk the local paths are soon rewarded with vistas largely unseen and unsuspected by those driving through on the B474. Despite its close proximity to High Wycombe, with which it is almost joined by continuous development, Penn, with its picturesque seventeenth-century inn and cottages clustered around its fine fourteenth-century church, has preserved a remarkably rural atmosphere. Though relatively small in size, Penn also attracts visitors from across the Atlantic as the village gave its name to an important Bucks family, from whom William Penn, the leading Quaker and founder of Pennsylvania claimed to be descended and it is indeed after his father, Admiral Penn, that Charles II named the state.

By the entrance to Grove´s Barn cross the B474 and take bridleway P52 bearing half right and passing right of the gates of Oakmead House to enter a green lane called Stumpwell Lane. Follow this gently downhill for 350 yards to enter a copse then at a fork by a woodland pond called Stump Well, bear right onto bridleway P57, also known as Stumpwell Lane. After 70 yards turn left over a stile onto path P58, bearing slightly right to pass through a gap in the bushes. Now bear slightly left across a meadow, passing right of an oak tree to cross a stile by a gate at the corner of a garden hedge, then follow this right-hand hedge straight on to reach a gravel drive at Beacon Hill (path P50). Beacon Hill, Penn, like other Chiltern hills with the same name, was one of a chain of beacon sites spanning the country which were used in 1588 to give warning of the approach of the Spanish armada.

Turn sharp left onto this drive, then, by the entrance to a cottage, bear right and take a path between hedges straight on to a stile into a field. Now follow a right-hand fence straight on across the field with a view of Penn Church to your left to cross another stile where fine views open out to the south across Burnham Beeches towards the distant North Downs. Here fork right onto path P51 along the outside edge of a wood ignoring a gate into it. In a corner of the field go straight on over a stile into and through the wood to a stile into another field. Now follow a left-hand hedge straight on to a stile into a wood called Coppice Hoop, through which you continue ahead for 300 yards to a fork near a corner of a field to your left. Here fork right, soon reaching the far corner of the wood, then (still on path P51) turn right over a stile and, ignoring the stile of a branching path to your left, follow the left-hand hedge straight on through two fields to cross a stile by a gate where a fine view opens out to your left towards the Wye Valley and Flackwell Heath.

Now take path P92 downhill bearing right and heading for the right-hand end of Sniggs Wood to cross a stile in the bottom hedge leading in a few yards to a crossing bridleway. Cross this ancient lane marking the parish boundary between Penn and Chepping Wycombe, bearing slightly left and taking path CW22c straight on uphill soon in a sunken way. On crossing a stile, bear left along the inside edge of the wood, soon bearing right and emerging onto the edge of a golf course. Now follow the left-hand hedge, soon bearing right then left, then, by a disused gate, ignore a branching path to your left into a strip of woodland and take a gravel track straight on along the edge of the wood to a junction of tracks on a rise where a fine view opens out to your left across the Wye Valley around Loudwater including the high brick viaduct built as part of the Great Western and Great Central Joint Railway in 1906.

Here bear slightly left and take the gravel track downhill beside a right-hand hedge. At a fork bear right into scrub. Soon after the scrub to your right gives way to the bank of a disused rubbish tip, fork left onto bridleway CW22b, a gravel track downhill out of the scrub to a track junction with views towards Loudwater. Here bear right onto a gravel track downhill to reach a crossing track (bridle-way CW27) near the golf course car park. Turn left onto this, then at a bend in the golf course drive, cross it and take the bridleway straight on behind a wooden barrier. At the far end of the barrier go straight on into the bushes where the bridleway becomes macadamed and you pass a gate. Ignoring a branching drive to your right, take the macadam drive straight on, later disregarding a branching bridleway to your right and rejoining the golf course drive. Here continue along its footway to its junction with Robinson Road where you bear half right, crossing Robinson Road and taking fenced bridleway CW27 straight on through woodland and under the railway viaduct. Now take a concrete road straight on downhill to a service road beside the A40 at Loudwater by a green with cherry trees which are a magnificent sight when in blossom.

Loudwater (Bucks.) - Flackwell Heath (Map 5)

Maps
OS Landranger Sheet 175
OS Explorer Sheet 172 (or old Sheet 3)
OS Pathfinder Sheet 1138 (SU89/99)
Chiltern Society FP Map No.13

Parking
Car park at King's Mead recreation ground.

Loudwater on the River Wye, as its name suggests, was once a village with watermills, but with its close proximity to High Wycombe with its furniture industry, the industrial revolution harnessed its water-power to drive papermills and other factories and workers' housing followed so that, by the early twentieth century, Loudwater had virtually become a suburb of the town with only the open expanse of King's Mead, an ancient common meadow, and the enclosing steep hills preserving the semblance of a gap between them.

Turn left onto the footway of the service road, joining the A40 then at traffic lights cross the main road and take Frederick Place over a bridge over one arm of the River Wye, immediately turning right onto macadamed path CW68 following a factory fence beside the River Wye onto King's Mead recreation ground. Here turn left and follow the left-hand fence round two sides of a floodlit rugby pitch, then bear left and follow a line of chestnut trees to a red-surfaced foot and cycle path. Turn right onto this, ignoring the first foot-bridge to your left and continuing (now on path HW53) until you reach a branching path leading to a second footbridge. Turn left onto this, crossing the other arm of the River Wye and reaching

Kingsmead Road, till the 1770s part of an ancient road from High Wycombe to Windsor, by the 'Papermakers Arms'.

Cross this road and take path CW30 up a concrete drive opposite crossing the course of the old GWR Maidenhead - High Wycombe branch line (opened in 1847, but largely superseded by the more direct GWR & GCR Joint Railway in 1906 and closed in 1970) and entering Fennell's Wood, named after the mediæval Fitz Neels who owned land in the Wycombe area. Now continue uphill along the inside edge of the wood ignoring all branching paths to your left. On approaching a tunnel under the M40, disregard a branching path to your right and take path CW53 straight on through the tunnel and up a flight of steps into the southern part of Fennell's Wood. Here ignore a branching path to your left and follow the M40 fence until you emerge into a field. Now turn left and follow the outside edge of the wood uphill, ignoring a branching path back into the wood, then continuing to a gate and stile. Cross this stile and follow the left-hand fence to the end of a macadam path between garden fences and a line of fence posts where there are fine views behind you across the Wye Valley towards the High Wycombe suburbs of Terriers, Totteridge and Micklefield. Take this path straight on, then, where it bears left and becomes fenced on both sides, fork right following a left-hand fence then crossing a stile into Oak Wood. Now keep left at a fork, then take a winding path through this wood keeping as close as possible to its left-hand edge, but disregarding a path into the housing estate, eventually reaching the far left-hand corner of the wood where you take the enclosed path straight on between garden fences and a hedge to reach a kissing-gate onto Heath End Road at Flackwell Heath.

Flackwell Heath - Sheepridge (Map 5)

Maps
OS Landranger Sheet 175
OS Explorer Sheet 172 (or old Sheet 3)
OS Pathfinder Sheets 1138 (SU89/99) & 1157 (SU88/98)
Chiltern Society FP Map No.13

Parking
On-street parking is possible in estate roads off Heath End Road, Flackwell Heath.

Flackwell Heath, (locally pronounced 'Flack'el'Eath') on its hilltop plateau separating the Wye Valley and High Wycombe from the Thames Valley to the south, was till the eighteenth century largely uninhabited. In the nineteenth and early twentieth centuries, however, a scattering of cottages and later ribbons of villas and bungalows gradually lined the Heath's network of lanes while, in between, there remained green fields and the vast cherry orchards for which Flackwell Heath became famous. It was not, however, till after the Second World War that the close proximity of High Wycombe and London and the scattered nature of the village's development made it a prime target for in-filling and expansion and the green fields and cherry orchards gave way to the large housing estates which characterise this suburban satellite of High Wycombe today.

Cross Heath End Road, turn right onto its far footway and follow it for 300 yards. Just past the junction with Spring Lane, by the entrance to no.159, turn left onto path CW38 along a narrow concealed alleyway between a hedge and a fence to a stile into a field. Now follow the right-hand hedge straight on downhill, soon on path LM24, with views ahead towards the Thames Valley around Cookham and Maidenhead. At the bottom end of the field go straight on through a hedge gap and join a grassy track, entering a sunken way and continuing downhill to gates into New Farm at Sheepridge. Now turn left to cross a stile into Sheepridge Lane, then turn right and follow it to the 'Crooked Billet'.'

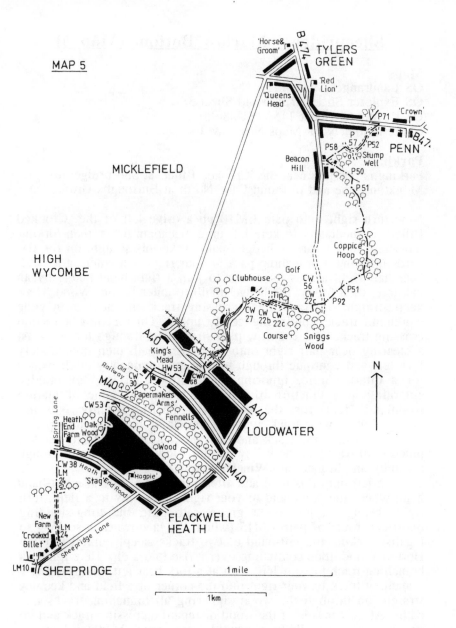

MAP 5

'Horse & Groom'

TYLERS GREEN

B.474

'Red Lion'

'Queens Head'

'Crown'

P71

P58 P57 P52

PENN

B.47.

Beacon Hill

Stump Well

P50

P51

MICKLEFIELD

Coppice Hoop

HIGH WYCOMBE

Golf

Clubhouse

CW 56

CW 22c

P51

Tip

P92

CW 27 CW 22b CW 22c

A40

Course

Sniggs Wood

King's Mead

CW 27

N

HW53

CW 68

Old Railway

CW 30

M40

A40

'Papermakers' Arms

Fennells

CW53

LOUDWATER

Heath End Farm

Oak Wood

Wood

M40

CW 38

LM 24

Heath End Road

'Stag'

Spring Lane

'Magpie'

New Farm

LM 24

FLACKWELL HEATH

'Crooked Billet'

Sheepridge Lane

LM10 SHEEPRIDGE

1 mile

1km

41

Sheepridge - Marlow Bottom (Map 6)

Maps
OS Landranger Sheet 175
OS Explorer Sheet 172 (or old Sheet 3)
OS Pathfinder Sheet 1157 (SU88/98)
Chiltern Society FP Maps Nos. 1 & 13

Parking
Parking is possible near the ´Crooked Billet` at Sheepridge, in Monkton Lane and in Pump Lane North at Burroughs Grove.

Now turn right onto path LM10 up a drive left of the ´Crooked Billet`, immediately forking left up a macadam drive, then forking left again into a narrow hedged path. Take this straight on for 100 yards ignoring a branching path to your right. On entering a field, bear half right across its corner to join a right-hand hedge by an oak tree, then follow the hedge uphill to enter Bloom Wood. Here keep straight on, ignoring a crossing track and now on a wide woodland track, continuing gently uphill. On reaching a second crossing track, take a narrow path straight on through the trees. At a clearing bear half right onto a crossing path then immediately fork left and continue through heathy, predominantly birch woods for a quarter mile, ignoring a crossing track and eventually emerging at a junction of wide tracks on the edge of mature woodland. Here cross the major track, bearing slightly right and taking another wide track, ignoring branching tracks at the top of a rise, then a crossing track and then descending steeply to reach a junction of tracks in the valley bottom. Now go straight on through a gap by an old gate into Winchbottom Lane.

Turn left onto this road and after a third of a mile at a left-hand bend where the woodland to your right gives way to a field, turn right through a gap by a green gate onto the long-standing unofficial route of path LM15 (which the landowner is seeking to legalise) taking the left-hand of two tracks steeply uphill through Horton Wood, then continuing over a rise into a dip. Here ignore a branching track to your left, then at a fork bear left, disregarding a branching track to your right into the corner of a field and keeping straight on through the woods ignoring all branching tracks and paths. At the far side of the wood disregard a crossing track and go straight on over a stile by a disused gate to reach Monkton Lane.

Here the **official route** turns left into Monkton Lane and follows it for over a quarter mile, passing under the A404, then, at a right-hand bend, turns right onto the old route of the lane and follows it for 300 yards past Wood Barn then uphill to reach a crossing drive, where you turn sharp left onto path LM13 passing the left-hand corner of a gas compound. If willing to risk crossing the A404 dual-carriageway, you can, however, save about 700 yards by taking **an alternative route**, which crosses Monkton Lane and goes straight on over a stile and up some steps to reach the A404 (Marlow Bypass). Here turn left, then level with a gap in the central-reservation crash-barrier, cross this fast dual-carriageway carefully and take path LM13 straight on over a stile by a gate opposite, following a concrete drive to a gas installation crossing the old course of Monkton Lane. Now bear half left passing the left-hand corner of the gas compound. **Both routes** now follow a sporadic left-hand hedge across a field with views through gaps in the hedge across the Thames Valley towards Cliveden, Winter Hill and Ashley Hill to reach an old gateway into Pump Lane North. Turn right onto this road and follow it to a T-junction with the old A404 near the 'Three Horseshoes' at Burroughs Grove.

Cross this busy road carefully and take path GM38a over a stile by an overgrown gate opposite, bearing slightly left across a field to a gap in the next hedge by an old stile just right of a copse with taller trees at Juniper Hill. Go through this gap and drop down into bridleway GM39. Turn left onto this then immediately fork right onto bridleway GM38, passing through the copse and emerging at the end of a stony lane by a cottage called 'Juniper'. Take this lane straight on downhill and up again to reach Hill Farm Road on the edge of Marlow Bottom.

Marlow Bottom - Bovingdon Green (Bucks.)
(Map 6)

Maps
OS Landranger Sheet 175
OS Explorer Sheet 172 (or old Sheet 3)
OS Pathfinder Sheet 1157 (SU88/98)
Chiltern Society FP Map No.1

Parking
On-street parking is possible in various roads in Marlow Bottom.

Though not planned like the new towns of Hertfordshire, Ordnance Survey maps from the 1920s show that Marlow Bottom is a new village which did not exist 100 years ago. In the 1920s and 1930s, however, the ribbon development, so deplored by the noted local writer, H.J. Massingham in his ´Chiltern Country` published in 1940, spread along its lanes and tracks to such an extent that post-war planners were unable to resist the pressure for ´in-filling` and now a village of some 5,000 inhabitants fills this once remote and reputedly picturesque winding Chiltern ´bottom`.

Bear half right across Hill Farm Road and take bridleway GM50 to the right of the entrance to no.65 along a narrow green lane which bears left. Now ignore a branching alleyway to your left and soon after the left-hand hedge gives way to a fence, fork right onto fenced path GM50a. On reaching New Road, cross it and take path GM50b straight on along another alleyway passing the end of a residential cul-de-sac to reach Beechtree Avenue. Turn left onto this road and after some 30 yards, just past house no.43, turn right onto path GM50c, a macadamed alleyway into and through woodland then steeply downhill between gardens to the road in the original Marlow Bottom which still bears this name.

Turn left onto this road then at a left-hand bend turn right onto path GM49 up a narrow alleyway, ignoring a crossing track and continuing along the edge of a recreation ground climbing onto a raised bank. At the top left-hand corner of the recreation ground turn right onto path GM43 following its top hedge to the edge of Whitehill Wood. Here ignore a bollarded gap into the wood and bear slightly right along the edge of the wood, soon entering the wood and following a slight sunken way along its right-hand edge. On reaching a crossing boundary bank, turn left then right and

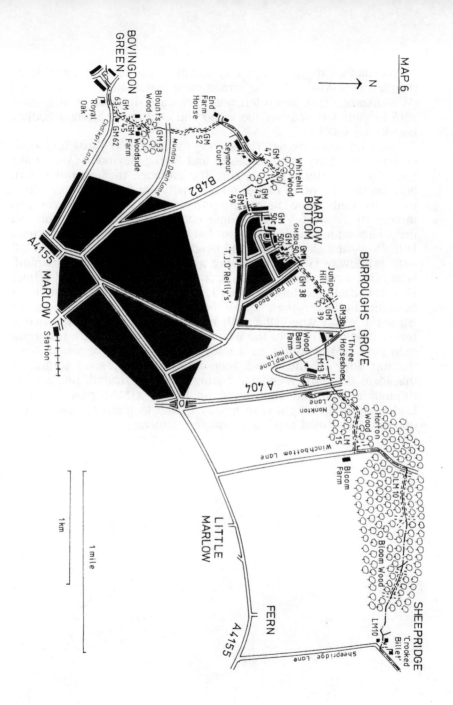

MAP 6

N

BOVINGDON
GREEN

'Royal
Oak'

GM
63

GM
45

GM
62

Woodside
Farm

Blount's
Wood

GM 53

End
Farm
House

GM
52

Seymour
Court

B482

Chalkpit Lane

Munday Dean Lane

GM
47

GM
41

Whitehill
Wood

GM
43

GM
49

MARLOW
BOTTOM

A4155

MARLOW

Station

GM
11

GM
50c

GM 50a 50

GM 50b

'T.J.O'Reilly's'

Juniper
Hill

GM 38a

GM 38

GM
39

Hill Farm Road

BURROUGHS
GROVE

Wood
Barn
Farm

'Three
Horseshoes'

Pump Lane
North

LM 13

A 404

Monkton
Lane

Horton
Wood

LM
15

Winchbottom Lane

Bloom
Farm

LITTLE
MARLOW

FERN

A4155

Sheepridge Lane

Bloom Wood

LM 10

LM 10

'Crooked
Billet'

SHEEPRIDGE

1 km

1 mile

45

follow another slight sunken way straight on to reach a gravel track (bridleway GM47) by the ornamental gates to a house called 'Woodlands'. Turn sharp left onto this track, ignoring a branching path to your left, leaving the wood and continuing along a hedged lane to the B482.

Turn left onto its nearside verge, then after 60 yards turn right crossing this busy road carefully and taking Seymour Court Lane for over a quarter mile, passing the entrance to Seymour Court, built on the site of an earlier house reputed to have been the birthplace of Lady Jane Seymour, one of Henry VIII's wives and mother of Edward VI, and some enormous ancient oak and ash trees, later with fine views to your left across Marlow towards Winter Hill. Now, at a sharp right-hand bend by End Farm House, turn left onto bridleway GM52, following a narrow sunken lane downhill, later with more views to your left across Marlow towards Winter Hill. On reaching Munday Dean Lane, take path GM53 straight on between bollards, then uphill between hedges to the edge of Blount's Wood where the path bears left and continues between fences along the edge of the wood. By a gate to your left, turn right onto path GM45 following a track uphill through the wood. Near the top edge of the wood keep left at a fork, soon joining a macadam drive by Woodside Farm. Follow it straight on, passing through a gate and continuing on byway GM62 past Blount's Lodge. Now fork right onto byway GM63 to reach Chalkpit Lane opposite the 'Royal Oak' at Bovingdon Green.

Bovingdon Green (Bucks.) - Hambleden (Map 7)

Maps
OS Landranger Sheet 175
OS Explorer Sheets 171 & 172 (or old Sheet 3)
OS Pathfinder Sheets 1156 (SU68/78) & 1157 (SU88/98)
Chiltern Society FP Maps Nos. 1 & 11

Parking
Little parking is available on this section except at Hambleden (see Map 8).

Bovingdon Green, on a hilltop above Marlow, whose Saxon name means ´green on the hill`, is a pleasant hamlet with most of its cottages clustered around the village green. Once boasting two pubs, one of which overlooked the green, the village still retains the ´Royal Oak` in Chalkpit Lane by an attractive duckpond.

Now turn right into Chalkpit Lane to reach the village green where you fork left across the green passing between wooden posts, soon crossing a road and continuing along a gravel track to the far right-hand corner of the green. Where this track bears left, leave it and go straight on across the grass and the end of a macadam road and take path GM10 along a gravelly flint lane to the left of the entrance to Cherry Tree Farm ignoring a branching path to your left. At the end of the lane take a fenced path straight on, then, after 150 yards, ignore a stile to your right and take path GM16 straight on for 350 yards, passing through two squeeze-stiles and a kissing-gate, then following the edge of Wolmer Wood to reach a wicket gate into Davenport Wood. Now keep straight on through the wood, after 200 yards disregarding a crossing path in a dip, then keeping left at a fork to reach a waymarked crossways in a second dip. Here turn right onto path GM15, going straight on through the wood and ignoring all branching tracks and paths, then, after 250 yards, keep right at two forks, soon bearing left to reach a road.

Cross this and take path M12 straight on, crossing a boundary bank, ignoring a branching path to your left and bearing slightly left. At a four-way fork bear half right, soon descending steeply, then, at the edge of the wood, disregard a crossing path and go straight on over a stile into a fenced path beside a right-hand hedge. Take this for a quarter mile to a stile into a field then turn left and follow the left-hand fence through two fields to a gate and stile onto a road on the edge of Homefield Wood. Turn right onto this road, then, in a dip, fork left through a gap by gates into the wood, taking the continuation of path M12 along a wide forestry track in the valley bottom for two-thirds of a mile ignoring all branching or crossing tracks or paths. After the valley and the track commence a long right-hand bend, look out for a track junction where you turn sharp left onto waymarked path M6, climbing through predominantly coniferous woodland to reach a squeeze-stile onto a road west of Bockmer End.

Turn right onto this road, then, after 150 yards turn left over a stile by a gate onto path M18. Having crossed a second stile by a gate into a field, go straight on across it, heading left of a cottage at Rotten Row ahead with fine views towards Bockmer and Ashley Hill to your left, to cross a stile in the next hedge. Now take path HA26b straight on to cross a stile right of a gate in front of a traditional black weatherboarded barn at Rotten Row, whose name seems likely to be an example of country humour referring to the one-time condition of its cottages.

Here take a concrete farm road straight on to reach a bend in a public road by an attractive duckpond, then take this road straight on, passing a fine half-timbered cottage with a flint extension and ignoring a branching path to your left. At a left-hand bend leave the road, forking right through a gate onto path HA26a which follows a grassy track between fields. On reaching a crossing stone track, take the grassy track straight on to the next hedgeline, then bear slightly right across a field to a corner of Rickoll´s Wood. Now follow the outside edge of the wood to a stile in the field corner leading into the wood. Here go straight on, soon joining a grassy track, then, at a T-junction of tracks, bear half right onto a grassy path downhill through the wood, eventually emerging from the wood by a corner of a field where fine views open out across the Thames Valley towards Mill End, Remenham Hill and Henley. Now follow the left-hand fence straight on downhill with Culham Court, a red-brick seventeenth-century Thames-side mansion on the other side of the river, emerging from behind some trees to your left.

On reaching a stony lane (path HA28), turn right onto it. After 100 yards, just before tall trees begin in the left-hand hedge, turn left through a hedge gap and take path HA26 straight on downhill to the corner of a hedge, then continue past it. Near a cottage turn right through a gate into a car park and go straight on through the car park to reach the end of a picturesque village street in Hambleden.

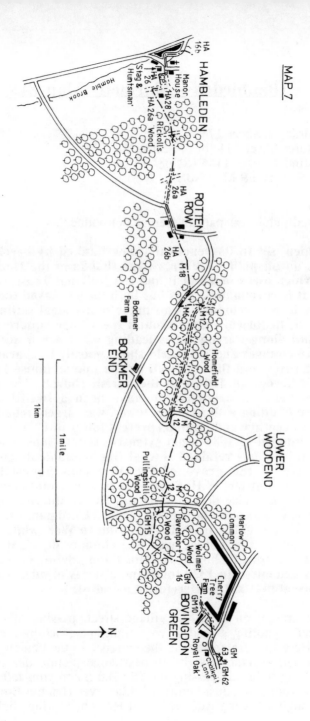

Hambleden - Skirmett (Map 8)

Maps
OS Landranger Sheet 175
OS Explorer Sheet 171 (or old Sheet 3)
OS Pathfinder Sheet 1156 (SU68/78)
Chiltern Society FP Map No.11

Parking
Signposted public car park in Hambleden village.

Hambleden, set in its beautiful valley flanked by beechwoods, remains an unspoilt Chiltern village thanks to the Hambleden Estate which owns much of it and the National Trust, to which most of it is covenanted. This has both largely saved the village from modern development and made it the ideal setting for a number of historical films. Around the village square with its pump and along narrow lanes leading off it are a number of attractive cottages and old-world shops, mostly in characteristic Chiltern brick-and-flint, as well as the manor house built for Emanuel Scrope in 1604 and the parish church. The church, which is believed originally to have been a twelfth-century cruciform building with a central tower, was largely rebuilt in the fourteenth century and given its present tower in 1721 which was then heightened in 1883 when extensive renovations took place. Despite this, it has retained several fine monuments and in its churchyard is the grave of the Victorian bookseller and government minister, W.H. Smith, the first Viscount Hambleden (1825 - 1891), whose descendants still live in the manor house. This house was also the birthplace of Lord Cardigan, who led the Charge of the Light Brigade in the Crimean War, while another famous son of the village was St. Thomas de Cantelupe, a thirteenth-century Bishop of Hereford and advisor of Edward I, who was canonised in 1320 following a series of miracles which took place at his tomb in Hereford Cathedral.

Now go straight on down the village street, passing the ´Stag & Huntsman`, ignoring a road to your right and reaching the village square. Here fork right, passing the entrance to the churchyard and taking a narrow lane straight on past some picturesque cottages, soon bearing right and passing the Old Bakery to your left and the church to your right. Just before a bridge over Hamble Brook, fork right through a kissing-gate onto path HA16b, bearing slightly left across a meadow, heading for the last cottage on a parallel road to your right to reach another kissing-gate, then go straight on across another meadow to a kissing-gate into a belt of tall trees near its right-hand end. Go through this tree belt then cross a stile and keep straight on, heading for the corner of a garden hedge by a walnut tree at Pheasant's Hill. Now follow this hedge straight on to a kissing-gate leading into a path between gardens, along which you continue until you reach a crossing macadam drive. Here go straight on, soon passing through a kissing-gate into a field and following a right-hand hedge straight on through two fields. At the far end of the second field go straight on through a hedge gap and follow a left-hand hedge, ignoring the stile of a branching path to your left and eventually reaching a kissing-gate near Colstrope Farm with its traditional Chiltern eighteenth-century brick-and-flint farmhouse. Now keep straight on to reach a kissing-gate onto the road through the hamlet of Colstrope, whose existence was first recorded in 1634.

Turn right onto this road, immediately bearing left, then, at a right-hand bend, take bridleway HA16a straight on along a green lane. On emerging into a right-hand field, continue along a sunken way beside a left-hand hedge, eventually entering a narrow green lane and following it straight on to a cul-de-sac road leading to The Hyde and Bagmoor.

Cross this road and a stile by a gate opposite and take a permissive path straight on across a field to cross the right-hand of two stiles by the right-hand end of a plantation, with fine views opening out ahead towards Skirmett and Cobstone Mill on a hill beyond. Now take path HA16 straight on across the next field, passing left of a chestnut tree to cross a stile in the next hedge. Here follow a right-hand hedge straight on past Flint Hall and Arizona Farm to your left, bearing left near the far end of the field to cross a stile into a fenced track. Now cross a stile by a gate opposite and follow a left-hand hedge to cross another stile at the far end of the field. Here bear slightly right, passing right of a hawthorn bush, then follow a sporadic left-hand hedge straight on. Where this hedge peters out, bear slightly left across the field, passing the corner of a right-hand hedge to cross a stile by a gate into Shogmoor Lane at Skirmett at the right-hand end of a flint wall.

Skirmett - Fingest (Map 8)

Maps
OS Landranger Sheet 175
OS Explorer Sheet 171 (or old Sheet 3)
OS Pathfinder Sheets 1137 (SU69/79) & 1156 (SU68/78)
Chiltern Society FP Map No.11

Parking
Limited on-street parking is available in Skirmett.

Skirmett, which has always been a hamlet of Hambleden parish, like nearby Fingest has the unusual distinction for this part of the country of bearing a Norse name meaning ´Shire meeting-place` although the Vikings only briefly penetrated this far south in the ninth century before being defeated and expelled by King Alfred. The village can boast an inn and some picturesque brick and flint cottages, but, despite its size and distance from the mother church in Hambleden, it did not have its own chapel-of-ease until 1886 and this has since closed and been converted into a private house.

Turn right into Shogmoor Lane and go gently uphill out of the village past some picturesque cottages. Just before a left-hand bend, turn left over a stile onto path HA14b going straight ahead to the corner of a hedge, then bear slightly left beside a fence to a field corner. Here turn sharp right onto path HA2c beside a left-hand fence to a stile, then bear slightly left across a field to a stile right of a gate into scrub, shortly emerging into a flint lane (bridleway HA2). Take this straight on uphill to a fork on the edge of Adam´s Wood, then continue uphill through the wood, ignoring a branching path to your left. Where the bridleway levels out, continue for a quarter mile. Soon after it climbs again, at a waymarked junction take path HA2b straight on uphill to a gate and squeeze-stile onto a fenced track (path HA1). Turn left onto this, ignoring a fork to your left and passing through a gap by a gate into a field. Bear slightly right across it to enter Fingest Wood by a wooden Hanger Estate sign. Now continue downhill through the wood to a gate and solid stile erected in memory of the noted walks writer Henry Fearon (1907 - 1995), better known by his pseudonym ´Fieldfare`, who loved the superb view from this point across Fingest towards Turville, Cobstone Mill and Ibstone ahead and Cadmore End and Bolter End on a ridge to your right. Having taken advantage of the nearby seat to admire this view, take the grassy track straight on downhill along the edge of the wood, later bearing right, crossing a stile by a gate and following a left-hand hedge to gates and a stile leading to a road on the edge of Fingest, onto which you turn left.

Fingest - Turville (Map 8)

Maps
OS Landranger Sheet 175
OS Explorer Sheet 171 (or old Sheet 3)
OS Pathfinder Sheet 1137 (SU69/79)
Chiltern Society FP Map No.11

Parking
Limited on-street parking is possible in Fingest.

The name Fingest, like Skirmett, is unusual as it derives from ´Thinghyrst`, a Norse name meaning ´meeting place in a spinney` and such names are usually only found in areas in the north and east held for longer by the Vikings. In the village the seventeenth-century ´Chequers Inn` is on your left, but of particular interest is the largely unaltered twelfth-century church with its unusually narrow lofty nave, thick plastered walls and tall Norman tower capped by a double saddleback roof, while in Chequers Lane to your right is the eighteenth-century village pound where stray animals were locked up to be redeemed on payment of a fine.

At a junction by the ´Chequers Inn` continue past the church to your right and at a left-hand bend, leave the road and take path HA61 straight on over a stile and along a fenced path by a flint wall, later continuing between fences to a corner of Mill Hanging Wood. Here at a three-way fork, bear left onto path I13, soon crossing a stile, a road and another stile opposite and continuing within a belt of trees round the contours of Turville Hill to your right. On emerging over a stile into a field, there are superb views of the picturesque village of Turville ahead, familiar to many television viewers as the setting for ´Dibley`. Now bear slightly left across the field with views to your right of Cobstone Mill, an eighteenth-century smock-mill which has featured in many films including ´Chitty Chitty Bang Bang`, to join a left-hand fence where it changes from wood to wire and follow it to gates. Here go through a kissing-gate then turn left over a stile by a gate onto path T30 down a flinty track between cottages into the centre of the village.

Turville - Southend (Bucks.) (Map 8)

Maps
OS Landranger Sheet 175
OS Explorer Sheet 171 (or old Sheet 3)
OS Pathfinder Sheets 1137 (SU69/79) & 1156 (SU68/78)
Chiltern Society FP Map No.11

Parking
Limited on-street parking is available in Turville, but do not use the pub car park without the landlord´s permission.

Although the name Turville has a French ring, it is, in fact, not of Norman origin, but a corruption of the Saxon name ´Thyrifeld´ (meaning ´Thyri´s field´) as the village is documented well before the Norman conquest. Indeed the church, whose fabric is in part eleventh-century but has a sixteenth-century tower and has undergone other substantial alterations over the centuries, is believed to have replaced a Saxon predecessor as it has a Saxon font. It is also associated with a gruesome mystery as, during renovation work in 1900, an old stone coffin was found hidden beneath the floor containing not only the skeleton of a thirteenth-century priest but also the remains of a seventeenth-century woman with a bullet hole in her skull! Apart from the church, the village can also boast a fine selection of sixteenth- to eighteenth-century cottages, some half-timbered and some brick-and-flint, as well as the picturesque timber-framed ´Bull and Butcher´.

Cross the village street and bear half right, passing left of the small green, then turn left into School Lane gently uphill. At the end of the road take bridleway T20 straight on between hedges to a bridle-gate into a field, then ignore stiles to right and left and follow a fence straight on. Disregard a bridlegate to your right and now on bridleway T1, follow the fence straight on for a third of a mile with fine views to your left towards Fingest and Skirmett and behind you of Cobstone Mill. On reaching gates into Dolesden Lane at Dolesden, cross this road, go through gates opposite and take a fenced track uphill, soon passing through a wood. At the far side of the wood, cross a stile by a gate and take a farm track straight on across a field with more fine views opening out behind you, to cross a stile by a gate at Southend Farm. Here take a macadamed farm road straight on past the farm, then continuing for a third of a mile to and across Southend Common to a T-junction.

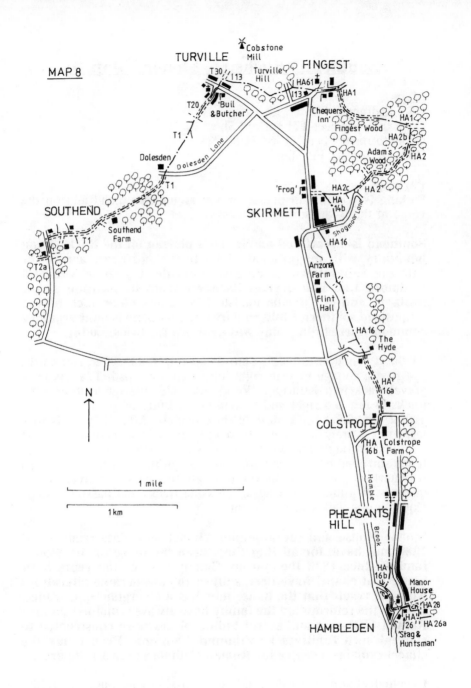

MAP 8

Cobstone Mill

TURVILLE   FINGEST

T30   113   Turville Hill   HA61
                                  113   HA1
T20   'Bull
      &Butcher'   Chequers
                           Inn'
T1   Fingest Wood   HA1

Dolesden   HA2b
                              Adam's   HA2
         T1   Wood

SOUTHEND   'Frog'   HA2c   HA2
                                 HA
                                 14b
              Southend
              Farm   SKIRMETT
      T1
                            Shogmoor Lane
    T2a   HA16

                     Arizona
                     Farm

                     Flint
                     Hall

N   HA 16
                            The
                            Hyde

                            HA
                            16a

1 mile
                     COLSTROPE
1 km
                     HA   Colstrope
                     16 b Farm

                     Hamble

                     Brook

                     PHEASANT'S
                     HILL

                            HA
                            16b
                            Manor
                            House
                            CR   HA 28
                            HA
                     HAMBLEDEN   26   HA 26a
                            'Stag &
                            Huntsman'

55

Southend (Bucks.) - Stonor (Map 9)

Maps
OS Landranger Sheet 175
OS Explorer Sheet 171 (or old Sheet 3)
OS Pathfinder Sheet 1156 (SU68/78)
Chiltern Society FP Map No.9

Parking
Parking is possible in places in and around Southend and on the verge of the B480 north of Stonor village.

Southend is a scattered hamlet on a plateau on the Bucks-Oxon boundary with magnificent views to the northeast across the Turville valley towards Fingest, Turville, Cobstone Mill and Cadmore End and derives its name from its location at the southern end of Turville parish. Like many other such hilltop outposts of southern Chiltern parishes, Southend is built around a common where hilltop clay was quarried for brickmaking.

At the T-junction turn left onto the public road. After 160 yards, just past a cottage to your right, turn right onto path T2a, taking a gravel track into Kildridge Wood. At a clearing ignore branching tracks to left and right and now in Oxfordshire on path PS10, take a flint woodland track straight on downhill. After 350 yards fork left onto a branching path, then keep right at a second fork and continue through the woods to a large kissing-gate in the deer fence surrounding Stonor Park. Go through this and follow a worn waymarked path straight on through the park for over three-quarters of a mile, ignoring all crossing tracks and passing Stonor House in the valley to your right.

Stonor House and the adjoining chapel both date from about 1280 and have, for all that time, been the home of the Stonor family (since 1838 the Barons Camoys). Over the years both house and chapel have been subject to considerable alterations with the result that the house now has a Georgian appearance. Despite the reformation the family have always remained staunch Roman Catholics and secret hiding places were constructed to conceal such fugitives as Edmund Campion. Even today the chapel remains a centre for Roman Catholics over a wide area.

Eventually path PS10 descends to a kissing-gate onto the B480.

56

Turn left onto this road and ignoring a branching road to Maidensgrove and Russell´s Water, continue into Stonor village.

Stonor - Maidensgrove (Map 9)

Maps
OS Landranger Sheet 175
OS Explorer Sheet 171 (or old Sheet 3)
OS Pathfinder Sheet 1156 (SU68/78)
Chiltern Society FP Maps Nos. 2 or 9

Parking
Parking is possible on the verge of the B480 north of Stonor.

Stonor, with its picturesque sixteenth- to eighteenth-century cottages and the eighteenth-century ´Stonor Arms`, was, till 1896, called Upper Assendon. As such, it completed the logical trio suggested by Lower and Middle Assendon further down the valley. However, with the establishment of modern local government, this former detached manor of the distant parish of Pyrton, whose main village and parish church are over five miles to the north near Watlington, initially became a separate parish and took the name of the Estate to which most of the parish belonged. Subsequently, in 1922, it was merged with the neighbouring parish of Pishill to form Pishill-with-Stonor. Its former name is, however, still preserved in Upper Assendon Farm with its seventeenth-century farmhouse at the southern end of the village.

At a right-hand bend turn right onto enclosed path PS12 between gardens to a stile into a field. Now go straight on uphill, passing left of an electricity pole to cross a stile in the top hedge. Here bear slightly left with superb views across the village behind you, passing just right of a copse. Now with views of Stonor House over your right shoulder, continue up the field to a stile into Park Wood by a tall ash tree, where you should turn round for fine views behind you. Here cross the stile and take the waymarked path straight on through the wood, ignoring all branching paths. At the far side of the wood, cross a stile and bear slightly left across a field heading for a tall conifer right of two cottages at Maidensgrove. By this tree turn left onto bridleway PS17, joining the Oxfordshire Way and taking a short green lane to the entrance to Lodge Farm, then turn right through the farm gates to reach the end of the village lane.

Maidensgrove - Park Corner (Redpits Lane) (Map 9)

Maps
OS Landranger Sheet 175
OS Explorer Sheet 171 (or old Sheet 3)
OS Pathfinder Sheet 1156 (SU68/78)
Chiltern Society FP Map No.9

Parking
Parking is possible on roadside verges near the entrance to SW31.

Maidensgrove, referred to in several late mediæval documents as ´Menygrove` (meaning a ´common clearing`) and described by the well-known Chiltern writer H.J. Massingham in 1940 as ´perhaps the most remote hamlet in all the Chilterns `, is the collective name for two small hamlets about three-quarters of a mile apart known as Maidensgrove and Upper Maidensgrove. Separated by part of the wide expanse of Russell´s Water Common, Maidensgrove is the larger with two farms and a number of cottages as well as several modern properties, while Upper Maidensgrove boasts a farm and a pub. Both the hamlets and the common are situated on a high ridge which affords extensive views over the surrounding hilltops and deep valleys.

Leaving the Oxfordshire Way, continue along the village lane for 300 yards, then, at a right-hand bend, fork left onto a gravel track leading out onto Russell´s Water Common. Ignore a branching track to your right, then, at a three-way fork, take the left-hand option and at a further fork go straight on along the back edge of the common to reach a bend in a macadam road. Here turn left into hedged flint lane SW31 ignoring gates to your left. Where the right-hand hedge ends by an old gate and views across the woods in Bix Bottom open out ahead, fork right onto path SW22 crossing a field, aiming just left of the corner of a wood called Big Ashes Plantation to reach a waymarked fence gap leading into it. Take an obvious waymarked path straight on within the top edge of the wood, eventually crossing a stile into another field. Bear half left across it, passing just right of an ash tree to cross a stile into a protruding finger of woodland. Now descend a long flight of steps through the wood to cross a stile at its bottom edge, then descend more steps into a field. Bear sharp right down this field, passing just right of a horse-jump to cross a stile by a gate in a corner leading

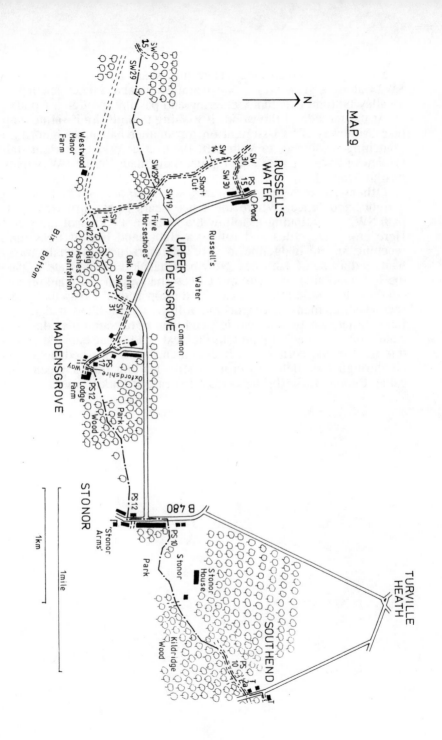

MAP 9

N

RUSSELL'S WATER

SW 29
SW 15
SW 15

Westwood Manor Farm

SW 30
SW 14
PS 15
SW 30
SW 29

Short Cut

Bix Bottom

SW 19

SW 14
SW 22
Big Ashes Plantation

'Five Horseshoes'

UPPER MAIDENSGROVE

Oak Farm

SW 22
SW 31

Russell's Water Common

MAIDENSGROVE

PS 17
Oxfordshire Way
Lodge Farm

PS 12 Wood

Park

STONOR

PS 12

'Stonor Arms'

B 480

PS 10

Park

Stonor House

Stonor Park

SOUTHEND

Kildridge Wood

PS 10

TURVILLE HEATH

1km

1mile

59

to a junction of green lanes. Here turn sharp right onto bridleway SW14 along a grassy track between a hedge and a fence leading up a valley bottom, eventually entering and passing through a wood.

At the far side of the wood, **if wishing to omit the Ewelme loop**, take bridleway SW14 straight on for another half-mile, ignoring a branching bridleway to your left, then, at a fork, bear right onto bridleway SW30 (Law Lane) rejoining the main Chiltern Way. Now turn to Map 11.

Otherwise, turn sharp left over a stile onto path SW21 following a right-hand fence. Where the fence bears right, turn right onto path SW29, continuing to follow the fence to a corner of the wood. Here cross two stiles and follow a right-hand line of trees until reaching an old hedgeline to your left marked by a small grassy bank and a line of ash trees. Now bear half left up the field to pass the left-hand side of a clump of trees shading an old chalkpit and continue to a stile left of a gate in the top hedge. Cross this and a second stile, then turn right and follow a right-hand hedge to a field corner, where you bear left and then right round the edge of a small copse to reach a gate into the next field. Bear half left across this field to the corner of a hedge, then follow this hedge straight on through two fields to cross a stile leading into a green lane called Redpits Lane (bridleway SW15) east of Park Corner.

Park Corner (Redpits Lane) - Ewelme (Map 10)

Maps
OS Landranger Sheet 175
OS Explorer Sheet 171 (or old Sheet 3)
OS Pathfinder Sheets 1137 (SU69/79) & 1156 (SU68/78)
Chiltern Society FP Map No.10

Parking
Small layby on B481 at Park Corner.

Turn left into Redpits Lane (bridleway SW15) and follow it to reach a bend in the village lane at Park Corner, which is so named as the hamlet is situated by the corner of what used to be Ewelme Park. Here fork right onto this road and follow it straight on to a T-junction with the B481. Cross this road and a stile opposite, then take path SW5 bearing left and following the back of the roadside hedge, eventually diverging away from the road and reaching a hedge gap into a wood called Springalls Plantation. Inside the wood, turn right onto crossing bridleway SW17, part of an ancient road from Henley-on-Thames to Oxford, following it through the wood, then along a green lane where you ignore a branching path to your left. On entering a second wood, take bridleway NE17 straight on, keeping right at a second fork, then ignoring a crossing track. On reaching a second crossing track, take bridleway NU7 straight on down a valley bottom for over a mile, passing through a bridlegate at one point then continuing along the middle of a belt of trees, crossing the Ridgeway and a grass track which links two fields, then passing a coniferous plantation to your left and eventually emerging at the far end of a tree belt. Here bear half left onto a farm track leading to a T-junction with a rough road (NU29), known as Old London Road as until the 1830s it was part of the London-Henley-Oxford turnpike road.

Turn right onto this road, soon passing a bungalow to your left. Now on EW37, continue past a left-hand copse. On emerging onto an open hillside, take the grassy track beside a right-hand bank straight on with wide views opening out ahead towards Wallingford and the Wessex Downs. After half a mile near the top of a rise, turn right through a gap in the grass bank onto bridleway EW29, passing the corner of a hedge. Now follow its right-hand side over Harcourt Hill where gaps in the hedge give views to your left on a clear day towards the Sinodun Hills and distant Oxford and

Ewelme Down and Swyncombe Down come into view ahead. Now continue beside the hedge downhill, eventually entering a copse concealing the ruins of Warren Farm. After about 80 yards, at the far end of a large gap in the left-hand hedge, turn left onto bridleway EW36, bearing slightly left over a rise. At the top of the rise, where a hedge comes into view ahead, aim for a corner of the hedge where the high hedge with trees to the right gives way to a low hedge to the left. Here turn right onto bridleway EW4, following a grassy track beside the hedge with fine views to your right towards Swyncombe Down and Ewelme Down. At a corner of the field go straight on through a hedge gap and joining the Swan's Way, take a fenced track, ignoring a farm road to your left by a barn. Here keep straight on along a green lane called Potters Lane (bridleway BN18/EW4) for over half a mile, eventually joining a concrete track and reaching a crossing road, part of the ancient Icknield Way.

Leaving the Swan's Way, turn right onto this road. After 30 yards, where a left-hand hedge begins, turn left onto bridleway EW17 known as Henley Way, passing the corner of a quarry fence, then continuing beside it with a deep gravel pit to your left, later with a second fence to your right, eventually reaching Day's Lane. Turn right onto this road with superb views of Ewelme opening out ahead, then immediately turn right again onto fenced path EW18, soon passing through a kissing-gate and following a left-hand hedge downhill to cross a stile into a belt of scrub. Continue through this, soon emerging onto a recreation ground, where you follow its left-hand edge straight on past a pavilion to reach Ewelme High Street by an iron gate (where the 'Shepherds Hut' is two-thirds of a mile to your left).

Ewelme - Swyncombe (Map 10)

Maps
OS Landranger Sheets 164 or 175
OS Explorer Sheet 171 (or old Sheet 3)
OS Pathfinder Sheet 1137 (SU69/79)
Chiltern Society FP Map No.10

Parking
Car parks at Ewelme Recreation Ground and Icknieldbank
Plantation.

Ewelme today is an idyllic sleepy Oxfordshire village with its cottages and old watercress beds nestling in the folds of the foothills of the southern Chiltern escarpment. The village became prominent in the early fifteenth century when the poet Chaucer´s son, Thomas, married the heiress to the manor and its fame was increased by their daughter Alice´s marriage in 1430 to William de la Pole, Duke of Suffolk. In the years which followed, the Suffolks completely rebuilt the church except for its recently-constructed tower and in 1437 they added thirteen almshouses built around a cloister in the fashion of Oxford colleges and a grammar school which is still in use as the village primary school and is believed to be the oldest primary school building in the country. The church contains a magnificent fifteenth-century carved oak font cover, an alabaster effigy of Alice Chaucer and her parents´ tomb with brasses depicting the poet´s son and one-time Speaker of the House of Commons and his wife, while Jerome K. Jerome, author of ´Three Men in a Boat` was buried in the churchyard in 1927. On the Suffolks´ downfall, the manor passed to the Crown and this resulted in the construction of a palace by Henry VII. This palace was later used by Henry VIII, whose bathing activities led to the pool at the head of the stream (more recently a watercress bed) being named King´s Pool. The palace also served as a childhood home to Elizabeth I but was later sold and allowed to decay so that only fragments of it have survived as part of the present Georgian manor house.

Turn right into Ewelme High Street, then, at a road junction, turn sharp left into Parson´s Lane (signposted to Britwell Salome and Watlington). After 150 yards at the top of a rise turn sharp right onto path EW23 along a flinty drive. At a fork take a grassy track straight on past a garden, soon becoming enclosed by a hedge to your right and a fence to your left. On emerging into a field with fine views ahead towards Swyncombe Down and Ewelme Down, bear slightly left across it to cross a stile in the next fence, then bear slightly left across a second field to reach a redundant stile at the next field boundary where there are superb panoramic views including the Sinodun Hills and Wessex Downs behind you. Now go straight on, heading towards what, at first sight, appears to be a triangular field on the side of Swyncombe Down, eventually dropping to a gate onto a bend in the Icknield Way road in Warren Bottom. Take this road straight on, then, after 350 yards just before the top of a slight rise, fork left through a hedge gap onto EW26. Now bear half right across the field, heading just right of an eighteenth-century obelisk in woodland at Britwell Park ahead to reach a junction of rough roads. Here turn right onto EW14 to reach a crossways with an unmade section of the Icknield Way and part of the Swan's Way near a corner of Icknieldbank Plantation.

Now take a rough road straight on for 35 yards, then turn left through a gap into the wood and take waymarked path SW37 bearing slightly right across open mature beechwoods. At the far side of the mature woodland take a worn path straight on uphill through scrubby woodland, eventually emerging near the top of Swyncombe Down onto one of the rare remaining areas of open downland in the Chilterns. Here take a grassy path straight on beside an ancient earthwork called the Danish Intrenchment, possibly dating from the abortive Danish attempts to conquer Southern England in the 870s A.D. which were ultimately repelled by King Alfred. On reaching the crest of the ridge, where fine views open out ahead along the Chiltern escarpment towards Watlington Hill, Shirburn Hill and Beacon Hill and to your left towards Britwell House, built for Sir Edward Simeon in about 1728, cross another earthwork and at a path junction by a metal gate, bear slightly right onto path SW36, passing through scrubland with a fence to your left and the Danish Intrenchment to your right and with fine views to your left in places. After over a third of a mile, where the fence bears away to your left, take a worn path straight on across open downland, eventually keeping right at a fork and climbing into Dean Wood to reach a T-junction with the Ridgeway (path SW4).

Turn right onto this, soon crossing the Danish Intrenchment and continuing uphill, ignoring branching tracks first to your left, then to your right. Having crossed the top of the ridge, continue downhill disregarding all branching tracks. On leaving the wood, keep straight on downhill along its outside edge, then uphill beside a right-hand hedge to a gate and kissing-gate leading to the junction of Church Lane and Rectory Hill at Swyncombe.

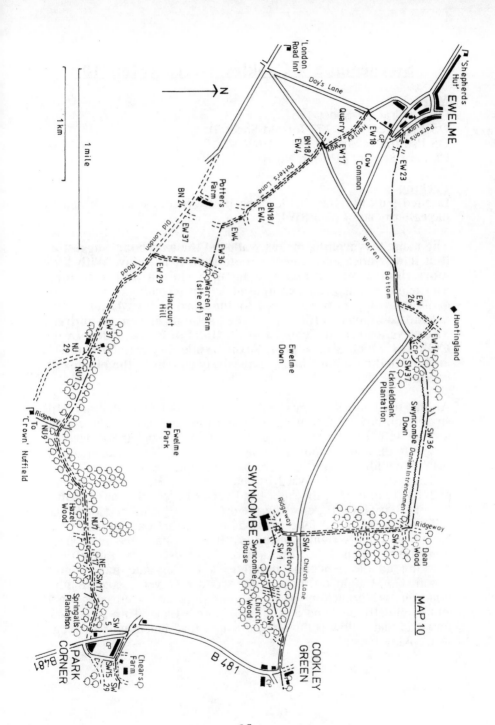

MAP 10

65

Swyncombe - Cookley Green (Map 10)

Maps
OS Landranger Sheet 175
OS Explorer Sheet 171 (or old Sheet 3)
OS Pathfinder Sheet 1137 (SU69/79)
Chiltern Society FP Map No.10

Parking
Limited parking is available opposite Swyncombe Church and by
the eastern end of path SW1.

**The name Swyncombe means ´valley of the wild boar` suggesting
that it was once even more remote than it is today. With little
more than a manor house, a farm, a church and a rectory,
Swyncombe is a good example of a ´closed village`, where the
ordinary villagers were forced by the Lord of the Manor to live
around commons on the edge of the parish or driven out entirely.
The eleventh-century church of St. Botolph is one of few in the
Chilterns which are, in part, Saxon, while Swyncombe House is
an Elizabethan manor house extensively rebuilt in the nineteenth
century.**

At the road junction cross Church Lane and take Rectory Hill
straight on downhill, bearing right at a fork and passing the church
to your left. By the far end of the church, leaving the Ridgeway,
turn left through a gate into the churchyard. Now take a gravel
path downhill past the church, bearing right by the church door
and leaving the churchyard by another gate. Here turn left onto
path SW1, following the right-hand edge of a clearing at first, then
keeping left at a fork, crossing the drive to Swyncombe House and
following a left-hand fence to a kissing-gate into a parkland field.
Now bear slightly right, passing just left of a lime tree and a large
elm stump, then following a slight depression in the ground
marking an old fenceline uphill to a kissing-gate into Church
Wood. Go straight on through the wood for over a quarter mile,
ignoring two branching paths to your right and a crossing track
and eventually crossing a stile into Church Lane. Turn right onto
this road and follow it for 300 yards to a road junction on the edge
of Cookley Green.

Cookley Green - Russell's Water (Map 11)

Maps
OS Landranger Sheet 175
OS Explorer Sheet 171 (or old Sheet 3)
OS Pathfinder Sheets 1137 (SU69/79) & 1156 (SU68/78)
Chiltern Society FP Map No.9

Parking
Small car park behind the village bus shelter on Cookley Green.

Cookley Green, with its large triangular green at the point where a number of ancient lanes meet, is today a picturesque village with a spacious feel which has suffered little from modern development. Like many villages with a green as their focal point, Cookley Green is not an ancient parish and has no church of its own, but grew up as a settlement to house the farmworkers and servants of Swyncombe Park, where the manor house, church, rectory and a farm are situated.

At the junction leave the road and go straight on across Cookley Green to its far end, then cross the B481 and turn left along its far verge. After a few yards by a large chestnut tree turn right into a gravel lane called Law Lane (bridleway SW30), ignoring the drive to Cookley House to your right and soon passing the house and a cottage. Now ignore the stile of a branching path to your left and continue gently downhill for half a mile, passing through a copse and eventually reaching a fork.

Here, **if wishing to take a circular walk on the Ewelme loop**, fork right onto bridleway SW14 and follow it down the valley bottom for half a mile, ignoring a branching bridleway to your right. On reaching the edge of a wood, fork right over a stile onto path SW21. Now go back to Map 9 for the continuation.

Otherwise, at the fork go left (still on bridleway SW30), soon bearing right and climbing steeply, then bearing left, levelling out and (now on bridleway PS15) reaching a road at Russell's Water, where the 'Five Horseshoes` at Upper Maidensgrove is half a mile to your right.

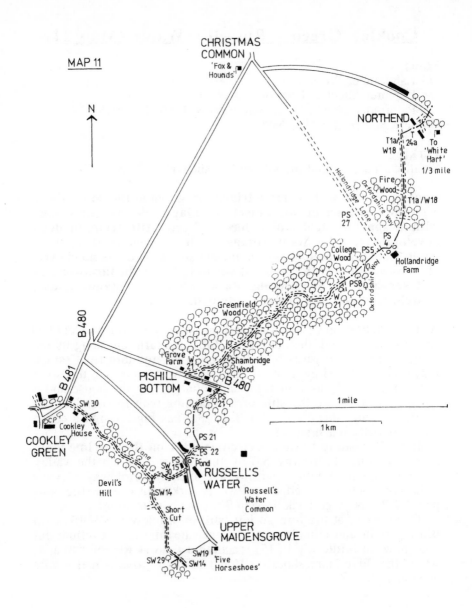

MAP 11

N

CHRISTMAS
COMMON
'Fox &
Hounds'

NORTHEND

T1a/   T   To
W18   24a   'White
Hart'
1/3 mile

Fire
Wood
T1a/W18

Hollandridge Lane

Oxfordshire Way

PS
27

PS
4

PS5

College
Wood

Hollandridge
Farm

70

PS8

W
21

Greenfield
Wood

B 480

B 481

Grove
Farm
W
21

Shambridge
Wood

PISHILL
BOTTOM

B 480

PS
21

1 mile

1 km

SW 30

CP

Cookley
House

COOKLEY
GREEN

Low Lane

PS 21

PS 22

SW 15

PS
Pond

RUSSELL'S
WATER

Devil's
Hill

Russell's
Water
Common

SW14

Short
Cut

UPPER
MAIDENSGROVE

SW19
SW29   SW14   'Five
Horseshoes'

Russell's Water - Northend (Map 11)

Maps
OS Landranger Sheet 175
OS Explorer Sheet 171 (or old Sheet 3)
OS Pathfinder Sheets 1137 (SU69/79) & 1156 (SU68/78)
Chiltern Society FP Map No.9

Parking
Parking bay west of Russell's Water Pond.

Russell's Water, which is named after a local brickmaker and his picturesque duckpond in the centre of the village, is a scattered community ranged along the edge of its extensive hilltop common on the ancient parish boundary between Pishill and Swyncombe. Its origins are obscure, but it is known to have existed since at least the late seventeenth century and it may occupy the site of a settlement called Pishill Venables which was recorded in the thirteenth century.

Turn left onto the road, rounding a left-hand, then a right-hand bend. Now by a triangular green with an old pub sign serving as a village nameboard, fork right onto a gravel track passing the attractive duckpond to your right, then fork right again. Just past the far side of the pond to your right and Pond Cottage to your left, turn left onto bridleway PS22. By the gates to Beehive Cottage, formerly the village pub, bear right and, ignoring branching tracks to left and right, continue until you emerge onto open common. Here turn left onto path PS21, following the edge of the common and ignoring gates to your left. After 350 yards at a corner of the open common, bear left into woodland and follow a waymarked path bearing right and continuing downhill, soon entering a slight sunken way. Eventually, by a huge beech tree, you leave the wood and continue down a cottage drive to the B480 in Pishill Bottom, the name of which, though being pronounced 'Pis-hill` with a short 'i`, is, in fact, a corruption of 'Peas-hill`.

Turn left onto this road and follow it for 350 yards, then turn right through iron gates onto bridleway W21 entering the farmyard of Grove Farm. Go straight across the farmyard, then, where a wire fence blocks your way ahead, bear right and immediately fork left onto a track beside the left-hand fence climbing into Shambridge Wood. On nearing the top of the rise, bear right and follow the waymarked track for 300 yards, ignoring all branching tracks. At a waymarked fork, take bridleway W21 straight on, descending into a valley where you ignore a crossing track, then climbing another rise. Now in Greenfield Wood, at a junction of tracks at the top of the rise, bear right, then keep left at two forks, descending again to reach a waymarked junction in the valley bottom. Here take bridleway W21 again, bearing half right, ignoring a crossing track and soon climbing again. At a fork keep right, soon bearing right into a mature plantation and following a winding waymarked track for a third of a mile, which later descends to reach a large clearing in another valley bottom.

Here bear slightly left, crossing the main track, then taking path PS8 straight on uphill through College Wood. Near the far side of the wood at a path junction, bear slightly left onto path PS5, joining the Oxfordshire Way and crossing a stile into a field. Now bear slightly right across a corner of the field to a corner of the right-hand hedge, then follow it straight on to a stile into Hollandridge Lane, a road dating from Saxon times which formed part of the spine road of the twelve-mile-long ancient strip parish of Pyrton stretching from Lower Standhill near Little Haseley in the Oxfordshire Plain to south of Stonor in the Chilterns.

Cross this unmade road and take path PS4 straight on along the edge of a copse concealing two ponds, gradually bearing left. At the far end of the copse, keep straight on across the field to a slight kink in the edge of a wood. Here bear left, crossing a concealed stile, then bear right, descending steeply to a crossways in the valley bottom. Now, leaving the Oxfordshire Way, take bridleway W18 straight on along a woodland track in the valley bottom for 350 yards, soon becoming T1a/W18 and straddling the Oxon/Bucks boundary and eventually reaching a bridlegate and fence gap into a field. Here follow the valley bottom straight on for a quarter mile, passing a solitary oak tree. Some 30 yards short of the corner of a fence, bear half right onto path T24a, entering Buckinghamshire and crossing the corner of a field to cross a stile in the fence. Now bear half right across a corner of the next field, heading just right of two white cottages to cross a stile into a narrow enclosed path between gardens. On emerging onto Northend Common, bear slightly left, crossing a gravel track and taking a mown grassy track through scrubland to rejoin the gravel track and reach a road.

Northend - Ibstone (Map 12)

Maps
OS Landranger Sheet 175
OS Explorer Sheet 171 (or old Sheet 3)
OS Pathfinder Sheet 1137 (SU69/79)
Chiltern Society FP Map No.9

Parking
Parking at Northend is now difficult, so that it is probably best to walk this section from Ibstone (see below).

Northend, with its scattered cottages spread unevenly around its extensive heathy and, in parts, wooded common, is justifiably popular with walkers owing to its attractive setting and the superb Chiltern views which can be obtained from surrounding footpaths. Although the village now straddles the Oxfordshire boundary, its name derives from its location at the northern end of the Buckinghamshire parish of Turville.

Cross the road and take an obvious grass path straight on through scrubland. On entering Blackmoor Wood by a Wormsley Estate sign and an old gatepost, where you cross back into Oxfordshire, take waymarked path SH8 straight on, descending gently at first and later steeply, then ignoring an old crossing track, levelling out and continuing on a track along the inside edge of the wood to a waymarked T-junction near New Gardens Farm where you should notice a short ha-ha ahead in front of a magnificent brick-and-flint wall and a large palladian stone ornament recently relocated in the wood to your left. Here turn right onto path SH4 following a green lane past the farm to reach a private road at the county boundary. Turn right onto this, reentering Buckinghamshire. Now on path S21, after 40 yards, fork left over a stile by a gate and cross the bottom corner of a field diagonally to a stile leading to another private road where fine views open out up and down the Wormsley Valley with the Stokenchurch telecom tower on the skyline to your left.

Most of the Wormsley Valley belongs to the Wormsley Estate, which, for over 400 years, was in the hands of one family, the Scropes and later, through female succession, the Fanes. It is thanks to them that no public road has ever been established through this beautiful valley and, in consequence, its natural

71

MAP 12

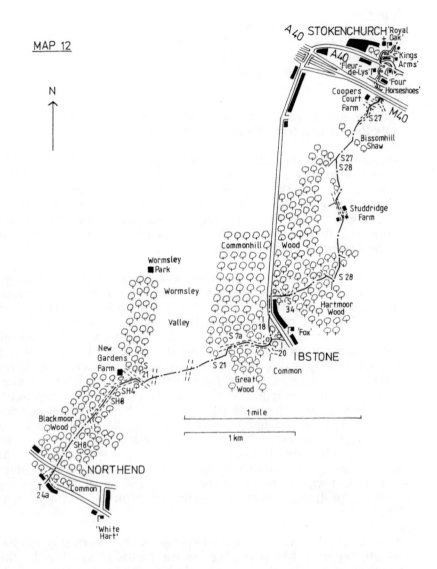

N

A40 STOKENCHURCH 'Royal Oak'
A40
'Kings Arms'
'Fleur-de-Lys'
'Four Horseshoes'
Coopers Court Farm
S 27
M40
Bissomhill Shaw
S 27
S 28
Studdridge Farm
Commonhill Wood
S 28
S 34
Hartmoor Wood
Wormsley Park
Wormsley
'Fox'
18
Valley
S 7a
20
IBSTONE
New Gardens Farm
S 21
SH4
SH8
S 21
Common
Great Wood
Blackmoor Wood
SH8
1 mile
NORTHEND
1 km
T 24a
Common
'White Hart'

peace and serenity have been preserved. In 1984, however, the Estate was sold to a holding company representing John Paul Getty Jr. and since then, large amounts of money have been spent on renovating the farms and cottages and not least Wormsley Park, its manor house of Palladian, eighteenth-century appearance but concealing some much older fabric, which is half a mile north of your present location. Extensive work has also been carried out on clearing and replanting the Estate's storm-ravaged woodlands, but it will be many years before their former glory has been restored.

Cross another stile opposite, then bear slightly left across a large field to cross a stile by gates onto bridleway S7. Now take path S21 straight on over a stile opposite and follow a left-hand fence uphill, passing through a clump of trees and bushes. Where the fence bears left, keep straight on along the edge of Commonhill Wood until the worn path bears left into the wood. Here turn round for a fine view back across the valley before entering the wood and climbing steeply to reach a T-junction with a sunken way (bridleway S7a). Turn right into this and follow it uphill. After 200 yards, where the bridleway levels out and a fine view across the Wormsley Valley opens out through the trees to your right, go straight on, ignoring a crossing track and following the inside edge of the wood, then a green lane to a T-junction on the edge of a scrubby part of Ibstone Common. Here turn left onto bridleway I18, soon passing a pond to your left. At a fork, **if wishing to visit the 'Fox'**, take bridleway I20 going right, then right again. **Otherwise**, fork left (still on I18), soon passing a second pond and continuing through scrubland for 200 yards to reach a bend in the road at Ibstone.

Ibstone - Stokenchurch (Map 12)

Maps
OS Landranger Sheets 165 & 175
OS Explorer Sheet 171 (or old Sheet 3)
OS Pathfinder Sheet 1137 (SU69/79)
Chiltern Society FP Map No.14

Parking
There are two parking bays at Ibstone opposite the ´Fox` and cars can also be parked along the western edge of the road to the north of this. Do not use the pub car park without the landlord´s permission.

Ibstone, scattered along more than a mile of lofty ridgetop separating the Wormsley and Turville valleys from Penley Bottom, until 1895 straddled the Bucks/Oxon boundary with its church, common and most of its cottages being in Oxfordshire, but, like neighbouring Stokenchurch, the village was then placed entirely within Buckinghamshire. While the origins of its Saxon name (spelt ´Hibestanes` or ´Ybestane` in the eleventh century) are uncertain, it may mean ´yew stone` referring to stones marking the old county boundary and the native Chiltern yew trees which seem to thrive on the shallow local soil. There is, indeed, a particularly fine ancient yew tree in the churchyard of Ibstone´s tiny twelfth-century church which also boasts a carved fifteenth-century wooden pulpit believed to be one of the oldest in the country and a Norman tub font. Being close to London, the village has, in modern times, attracted a number of well-known residents including the authoress Dame Rebecca West who lived at the imposing neo-classical eighteenth-century Ibstone House.

Cross the road and turn left along its far verge. On reaching the entrance to the last cottage, turn right through two gates onto path S34, bearing slightly right and following a right-hand fence to a gate into Commonhill Wood. In the wood take the waymarked path straight on, ignoring a crossing track and a branching track to your left. Now follow the inside edge of the wood at first before continuing downhill through the wood. In the valley bottom bear right to reach a path junction by the corner of a field. Here bear left through a hedge gap and take path S28 following the outside edge of the wood uphill. Just before the top corner of the field, turn left through a waymarked fence gap and take a winding

74

waymarked path generally uphill through scrubby woodland. On emerging into a young plantation, turn left at a path junction (still on path S28) and follow a left-hand hedge uphill through the plantation and two fields to Studdridge Farm, with fine views over your right shoulder in places down Penley Bottom and the Hambleden Valley towards the distant Thames and Bowsey Hill in Berkshire.

At Studdridge Farm, go through a kissing-gate and take the macadam drive straight on, passing left of most of the buildings and continuing to the far end of a line of trained fruit bushes enclosing the garden. On passing through a gate, turn right over a stile by a gate with views towards Stokenchurch and the M40 ahead, then bear half left across the field to pass the right-hand end of a copse concealing two ponds. Now bear slightly left and follow the edge of this copse to its far end where you bear slightly right across the field, aiming to the left of three trees, to reach the far corner of the field. Here cross a stile by a New Zealand (barbed-wire) gate and take path S27, following a left-hand hedge gently downhill towards a pair of timber gateposts, where you cross a concealed stile into Bissomhill Shaw. Now take a fenced track downhill through this wood to cross a stile and footbridge in the valley bottom, then follow a left-hand hedge straight on uphill to cross a stile into a fenced cattle track. Take this track straight on to a junction of tracks by Coopers Court Farm where you cross a cluster of three stiles with farm buildings to your left, then bear right across the field to a stile without a top rail leading in 25 yards to a junction of farm roads. Here turn left and take the fenced path through the left-hand side of the M40 underpass, then bear left up a macadam farm road to reach a road junction. Now take Coopers Court Road straight on uphill to Stokenchurch village green where you go straight on, passing left of two large grass ´traffic islands` to reach the A40 virtually opposite the ´Kings Arms`.

Stokenchurch - Radnage (Map 13)

Maps
OS Landranger Sheet 165
OS Explorer Sheet 171 (or old Sheet 3)
OS Pathfinder Sheet 1137 (SU69/79)
Chiltern Society FP Maps Nos. 7 & 14

Parking
Large public car park outside the ´Kings Arms Hotel`, Stokenchurch.

Stokenchurch, on the London-Oxford road on a ridgetop plateau about a mile from the escarpment and one of the highest major settlements in the Chilterns, has the unfortunate reputation of being ´the ugly duckling` of the Chilterns. This may arise from its former role as a centre of the Bucks furniture industry with its factories and timber yards or from the extent to which it has been developed for housing since the coming of the M40. Nevertheless the village, only transferred from Oxfordshire to Bucks in 1896, can boast extensive, attractive, well-maintained village greens where an annual horse fair used to be held on July 10th and 11th and a funfair is still held to this day. The twelfth-century parish church, hidden behind the ´King´s Arms ,` is quite sizeable when one considers that, until 1844, it was merely a chapel-of-ease for Aston Rowant and, despite many renovations, it is still worth a visit. This is also the burial place of Hannah Ball (1734-1792), a friend of John Wesley and founder of the first English Sunday school in High Wycombe in 1769. For the walker, however, the chief attraction of Stokenchurch is that it is an ideal centre for exploring some of the finest Chiltern countryside including the Wormsley Valley, Penley Bottom, Radnage and the escarpment.

Cross the A40 bearing slightly left and take Church Street, bearing right by Lloyds Bank and passing the church. At a crossroads by the ´Royal Oak`, turn left into Park Lane. Where the public road ends by the entrance to Longburrow Hall, take path S92 straight on along a private road past a sporadic line of ancient chestnut trees. At the far end of the trees, turn right through a kissing-gate by several gates onto path S79 beside a left-hand fence. Where the fence ends, follow a sporadic line of trees straight on to a kissing-gate, then bear half left, passing an electricity pole and aiming for the end of a hedge right of a bungalow. Here bear half right onto path S80 along a flint track. Where the track wiggles to the right and a left-hand hedge begins, turn left through a hedge gap then right and follow the hedge straight on through two fields with fine views ahead towards Bennett End in the valley and Bledlow Ridge beyond. At the far end of the second field, bear right through a hedge gap and descend some steps. Now bear left across a farm track and down more steps and aim for a thornbush right of a line of four trees in the valley bottom. Here turn right onto bridleway S87, part of an ancient road to Oxford on the Bucks/Oxon boundary known as Colliers Lane, as it was, at one time, used by Welsh colliers to transport coal to London.

After 70 yards by a waymarking post, bear half left onto path CR10 entering the tip of a salient of Oxfordshire, soon crossing a stile and continuing to a second. Now bear right to reach a farm track, onto which you bear left. After 20 yards turn right through a concealed hedge gap into Grange Farm Road reentering Bucks. Now take path RA16 through a hedge gap opposite and bear half left up the field aiming for an electricity pole in the top hedge. Here turn left and follow the hedge uphill to a gap in the top corner where there is a fine view back towards Stokenchurch. Now go through the hedge gap and turn right over a concealed stile, then follow the right-hand hedge uphill to a stile and gates. Cross this stile, a drive and a stile by gates opposite, then bear half right onto path RA17 along the macadam drive to Andridge Farm.

At the first fork keep left, passing left of a bungalow, then, at a second, go straight on, soon entering a field. Here, if wishing to visit the 'Three Horseshoes` at Bennett End, bear half right onto path RA14, at the bottom of which the pub is to your right. Otherwise, bear slightly left onto path RA13, following a left-hand hedge downhill with a superb view ahead down Radnage Bottom towards West Wycombe Hill capped by St. Lawrence's Church, a thirteenth-century church extensively rebuilt in 1763 by Francis Lord le Despencer (formerly Sir Francis Dashwood of Hellfire Club fame) who added to its tower the golden ball for which it is famous.

At a corner of the field go through a hedge gap to cross a concealed stile and take the enclosed path downhill to Horseshoe Road. Turn left onto this downhill to a road junction in Radnage Town End, then turn left into Town End Road. At a left-hand bend turn right through a fence gap onto path RA5, following a left-hand hedge to cross a gravel drive and a stile, then keep straight on towards Radnage Church to cross a stile in a field corner. Now cross Church Lane and take the church drive straight on uphill. Where the drive bears left, take path RA6 straight on through a gate and up a path to the church door.

Radnage - Bledlow Ridge (Map 13)

Maps
OS Landranger Sheet 165
OS Explorer Sheet 171 (or old Sheet 3)
OS Pathfinder Sheet 1137 (SU69/79)
Chiltern Society FP Map No.7

Parking
Little parking is available on this section except at Bledlow Ridge (see below).

Radnage, whose name is a corruption of ´Radenach`, meaning ´red oak`, as it was recorded in the twelfth century, is a very scattered community comprising quite a number of separate hamlets, but the bulk of its population today lives on the ridge to the south of Radnage Bottom where the hamlets known as The City, Radnage Common and Green End have virtually been joined together by pre-war ribbon development of the type so deplored by the contemporary Chiltern writer, H.J. Massingham. Aerial photographs have, however, revealed that the eighteenth-century former rectory and the thirteenth-century church, notable for its unusual central tower, its Saxon font dug up in a nearby field and a thirteenth-century mural discovered beneath later murals during restoration work, once formed the nucleus of a larger settlement, but the reasons for its disappearance are unknown.

By the church door, take path RA6, bearing half right, passing a seat and continuing to the far side of the churchyard. Here cross stone and wooden stiles and bear half right across a field to cross another stile, then continue across a further field to cross a stile by a gate. Now take path B66a bearing half left uphill to cross a stile in the top corner of the field by the edge of Yoesden Wood (the name of which is thought to be a corruption of ´yews-dene`), then follow a right-hand fence uphill. Where the fence bears right, follow it, then soon take a worn path bearing left and climbing steeply up the left side of a scrubby field, entering Yoesden Wood and continuing over a stile to reach a fork at the far side of the wood. Here turn left onto path B66 and follow it uphill between a hedge and a fence with fine views to your right in places, to reach Chinnor Road, the ridgetop spine road of Bledlow Ridge.

Bledlow Ridge - Wigan's Lane (Map 13)

Maps
OS Landranger Sheet 165
OS Explorer Sheet 171 (or old Sheets 2 & 3)
OS Pathfinder Sheets 1117 (SP60/70) & 1137 (SU69/79)
Chiltern Society FP Map No.7

Parking
Limited on-street parking is available in places at Bledlow Ridge and Rout's Green.

Bledlow Ridge village, most of which stretches along one and a half miles of the high steep-sided ridge of the same name, was described by the Chiltern writer, H.J. Massingham in 1940 as 'the bastard village` as he saw it as a particularly conspicuous manifestation of the pre-war ribbon development which was threatening to ruin the Chilterns. However, while there undoubtedly was a rash of pre-war building at Bledlow Ridge, the first edition Ordnance Survey map of 1822 already reveals clusters of scattered development along the ridge, which in 1868 was sufficient to justify the building of a church. Some of its cottages, indeed, even date from the seventeenth century, when a battle appears to have taken place there in 1643 during the Civil War as numerous weapons dating from that period have been found including a sword hidden in a chimney at Pankridge Farm.

Cross Chinnor Road and take path B62 straight on along a gravel lane, soon bearing left. Where the lane ends, bear slightly left along a path between a hedge and a fence to reach a gate and stiles. Here ignore the stile to your right and turn left, crossing a second stile. Now continue with a hedge to your left and fine views ahead towards Lodge Hill, a strange-looking single hill in the Saunderton valley where neolithic tools and bronze age burial mounds and pottery have been found, and to your right across the valley towards Whiteleaf Cross, a chalk cross carved into the hillside of unknown origin, Loosley Row and Lacey Green. Later cross a further stile and continue to Chapel Lane (path B61). Turn right into this downhill, then, just before a gate and stile, turn left over a stile onto the continuation of path B62. Go straight ahead, passing a cottage to your right, then keep left of a hedge, going through a hedge gap and continue to follow the right-hand hedge to a stile. Now descend a steep bank to a kissing-gate, then follow the right-

79

hand hedge, then the edge of a copse downhill and up again to cross a stile and follow an enclosed path to a road at the hamlet of Rout's Green (bridleway B57).

Turn left onto this road, then, at a T-junction, turn right onto bridleway B56. Where its macadam surface ends, bear left onto its stone continuation to reach the edge of Neighbour's Wood. Here continue into the wood and follow its inside edge straight on downhill. On leaving the wood, continue along an ancient green lane with close-up views of Lodge Hill to your right when the right-hand hedge becomes lower and finally peters out. On reaching a crossing track, where, at the time of writing, the landowner is seeking a controversial diversion of the bridleway, you currently go straight on along a sunken green lane to Callow Down Farm. Here continue along a concrete road with the thatched, half-timbered farmhouse to your left and farm buildings to your right. At the far side of the farm by a wooden building with a green tank (where the proposed diversion would rejoin the current route), bear slightly right to follow a left-hand line of trees, soon entering a green lane and continuing along it past Old Callow Down Farm with its early seventeenth-century, half-timbered farmhouse with lattice windows. Just past the farm, join its drive and follow it straight on, soon bearing left and, now on path B84, continuing with fine views to your right towards Whiteleaf Cross and to your left over the remote country near Bledlow Great Wood, to reach Wigan's Lane.

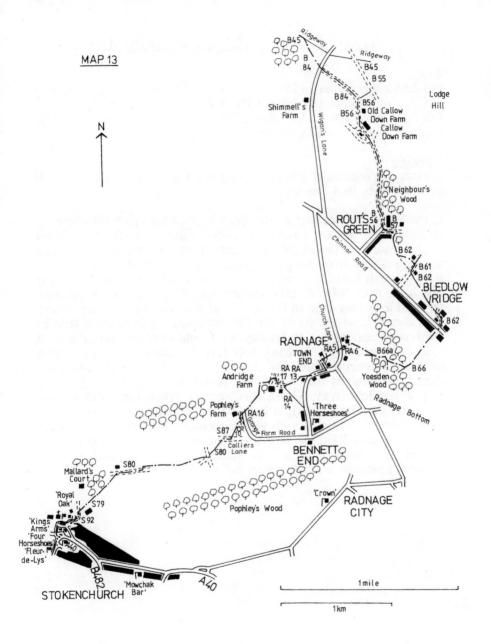

MAP 13

N

Ridgeway
B 45
B 84
Ridgeway
B45
B 55
Shimmell's Farm
B 84
B56
B56 ■ Old Callow Down Farm
Callow Down Farm
Lodge Hill

Wigan's Lane

Neighbour's Wood

ROUT'S GREEN
B 56
B 57
B 62
B 61
B 62
BLEDLOW RIDGE
B 62

Chinnor Road

Church Lane

RADNAGE
TOWN END
RA5
RA 6
B66a
B 66
Yoesden Wood
Radnage Bottom

Andridge Farm
RA RA 17 13

Pophley's Farm
RA16
RA 14
'Three Horseshoes'

S87
GR
Grange Farm Road
Colliers Lane
S80

BENNETT END

Mallard's Court
S80
Pophley's Wood
'Crown'
RADNAGE CITY

'Royal Oak'
S79
'Kings Arms'
S 92
'Four Horseshoes'
'Fleur-de-Lys'
A40
B482
'Mowchak Bar'
A40
STOKENCHURCH

1 mile

1 km

81

Wigan's Lane - Bledlow (Map 14)

Maps
OS Landranger Sheet 165
OS Explorer Sheet 181 (or old Sheet 2)
OS Pathfinder Sheet 1117 (SP60/70)
Chiltern Society FP Maps Nos. 7 or 14

Parking
Parking is possible at a bend in Wigan's Lane a quarter mile north of where path B84 crosses it.

Cross Wigan's Lane and a stile opposite, then take path B84 bearing slightly right across a field to cross a stile in its far right-hand corner leading to the Ridgeway, where there are superb views ahead across Princes Risborough towards Whiteleaf Cross and to your right towards Loosley Row, Lacey Green and Lodge Hill. Now turn left onto path B45, briefly joining the Ridgeway, soon passing through a kissing-gate in the left-hand fence and continuing along the other side of the fence for 150 yards until you reach a stile in the fence. Leaving the Ridgeway, turn right over this and a second stile onto path B22, bearing half left downhill to a stile into a thicket. Go steeply uphill through the thicket to cross another stile, then keep straight on over a rise to reach a stile leading to the Upper Icknield Way. Cross this ancient green lane and a stile opposite, then follow a right-hand hedge straight on for over half a mile through two fields with views opening out ahead at the top of a rise towards Bledlow and the Vale of Aylesbury beyond. On reaching the backs of gardens at Bledlow, cross a stile and continue between fences to a village street called Church End.

Bledlow - Saunderton (Map 14)

Maps
OS Landranger Sheet 165
OS Explorer Sheet 181 (or old Sheet 2)
OS Pathfinder Sheet 1117 (SP60/70)
Chiltern Society FP Map No.7

Parking
Parking area on either side of the telephone box in Church End, Bledlow between the church and the 'Lions`.

Bledlow, on the lower slopes of Wain Hill where the Risborough gap in the Chiltern Hills meets the Vale of Aylesbury, is now a picturesque Chiltern backwater, but it has an obviously strategic location and a history to match. Evidence of settlement in the Bronze Age has been found in nearby woods, but references to the village itself go back at least a thousand years. Its name, recorded in 1012 as 'Bleddanhlæw`, though undoubtedly of Anglo-Saxon origin, is variously said to mean 'Bledda´s Hill` or 'Bloody Hill`, the latter interpretation being thought to refer to a battle near the village between the Saxons and the Vikings and in 1066, it is thought to have been visited and sacked by William the Conqueror´s army. Bledlow today can boast a largely unaltered thirteenth-century church with a carved Norman font, fourteenth-century murals and heraldic glass and nearby are some attractive sixteenth-century timbered cottages with herringbone brickwork and the early eighteenth-century manor house which, since 1801, has belonged to the Carringtons.

Turn right into Church End and follow it past the cottages with herringbone brickwork, the church, a ravine containing a brook called The Lyde and the manor house to a T-junction opposite a former children´s home. Here turn right, then, after 200 yards, just past the last left-hand house, turn left through a bridlegate onto bridleway B23, bearing slightly right across a field and heading towards an electricity pylon on the skyline, to reach a gap in the far hedge leading into Old Oddley Lane (byway B91), a green lane probably of Saxon origin following the ancient parish boundary between Bledlow and Saunderton. Turn right into this lane, then, after 70 yards, fork left through a hedge gap onto path B35, bearing slightly right and following what is normally a crop break to the right-hand end of a hedge by a twin-poled pylon. Here bear slightly left, soon joining a farm road by Frogmore Farm with its fifteenth-century brick-and-timber farmhouse and following it straight on to a bend in a road called Oddley Lane. Now take this road straight on to a T-junction in Saunderton.

Saunderton - Lacey Green (Map 14)

Maps
OS Landranger Sheet 165
OS Explorer Sheet 181 (or old Sheet 2)
OS Pathfinder Sheets 1117 (SP60/70) & 1118 (SP80/90)
Chiltern Society FP Map No.7

Parking
Limited on-street parking is available at Saunderton and Loosley Row.

Saunderton comprises several small hamlets spread along the valley and for some strange reason, the original village with its church, where you now are, is much closer to Princes Risborough Station than to Saunderton Station, nearly three miles to the southeast! The thirteenth-century church, originally one of two suggesting that, in the Middle Ages, Saunderton was a place of some importance, was extensively restored in the nineteenth century, but retains its original font, an ancient brass and mediæval tiles, while nearby is the moat of a Norman castle and in a field to the east is the site of a Roman villa.

At the T-junction, turn left into Bledlow Road, then, by a postbox, turn right into Church Lane, passing two ornamental lakes. After 75 yards, virtually opposite the drive to Church Farm House, turn left onto path B83, following a concrete path to gates into the churchyard. Now take a grassy path straight on across the church-yard to a kissing-gate leading into marshy woodland concealing the old castle site. Here go straight on until you emerge into a field, then turn right onto path B37, following a right-hand hedge until a stile and flight of steps lead you to the Birmingham-bound track of the Chiltern Line on the course of the original single-tracked Wycombe Railway, extended in 1862 from High Wycombe to Thame. Cross the railway carefully, then descend its bank to cross another stile and follow the right-hand hedge straight on. Where the hedge ends, bear slightly left across the field to the near left-

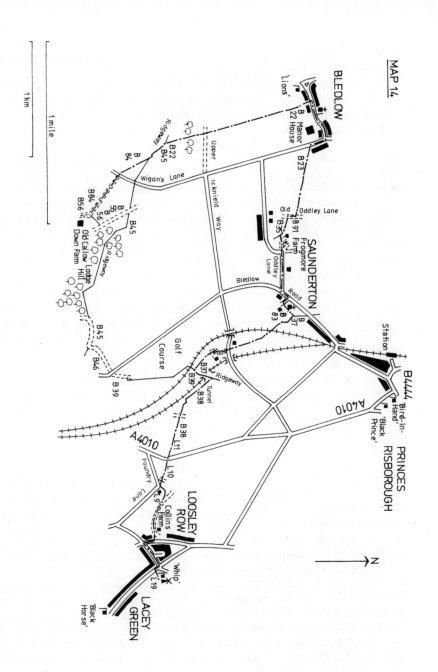

MAP 14

BLEDLOW

'Lions'

B22 Manor House

B23

Ridgeway

B22
B45

B
B4

Upper

Wigan's Lane

Icknield Way

B84
B56

B
56
55

B45

Old Callow Lodge
Down Farm
Hill

Ridgeway

Old Oddley Lane

B35 B91

Frogmore Farm

SAUNDERTON

Oddley Lane

Bledlow

Road

B
B37

83

Station

B45

Golf Course

B46

B39

Ridgeway

B37
B39

Tunnel

B38

B38

L11

A4010

Foundry Lane

L10

L9 Collins Farm

LOOSLEY ROW

'Whip'
L19

LACEY GREEN

'Black Horse'

B4444

Bird-in-Hand'

'Black Prince'

A4010

PRINCES RISBOROUGH

N

1km

1mile

85

hand corner of a garden hedge, then follow this hedge straight on to a gap leading to a road section of the ancient Upper Icknield Way (beware - poor visibility!)

Cross this road and take path B37 straight on through the gates of The Old Rectory and along its drive, bearing right then left. Where the drive bears left again, leave it and follow the right-hand hedge straight on to a gate and stile into a field. Here bear slightly left over a slight rise, soon aiming for a clump of hawthorn trees ahead, where you turn left onto path B39, briefly joining the Ridgeway, passing right of a line of trees, then bearing slightly left uphill to a kissing-gate. Now go straight on through a belt of scrub above the mouth of a tunnel on the London-bound track of the Chiltern Line, built when the line became double-tracked and the direct line to Marylebone and Paddington opened in 1906. On reaching another kissing-gate, go through it, then, leaving the Ridgeway, turn right onto path B38, following a right-hand hedge for 400 yards above the railway cutting with fine views to your left across the valley towards Whiteleaf Cross, Loosley Row and Lacey Green. Having wiggled to the left at one point, level with a twin-trunked oak tree in the sporadic hedge to your left, turn left across the field to this oak tree, where you cross a track and keep straight on across the next field (soon on path L11) to reach a kissing-gate in the far corner of the field leading to the A4010.

Before passing through the kissing-gate, turn round for a fine view back towards Lodge Hill and Wain Hill, then go through the gate, cross the main road and take path L10 straight on through a hedge gap opposite. Now follow a right-hand fence until you reach a crossing track. Here go straight on through a plantation to a hedge gap by some tall cypress trees leading to Foundry Lane. Do **not** go through this gap, but turn left onto path L9, following a right-hand hedge with fine views over your left shoulder towards Lodge Hill, Wain Hill and the Vale of Aylesbury beyond. Where the hedge bears right, join a farm track and follow it gently uphill, soon enclosed by hedges and later fences. By some farm buildings, join a concrete road and follow it straight on uphill, soon bearing left. Before reaching a gate, fork right up a fenced path to reach a kissing-gate leading to Lower Road in Loosley Row.

Although it has sometimes been speculated that the name Loosley Row is an example of local humour referring to the straggling nature of the hamlet, experts believe it to come from the Saxon ´hlose-leah` meaning ´pigsty clearing`, suggesting what it may have been like a thousand years ago. Turn right onto this road passing the Baptist Chapel. At a crossroads, turn left up Loosley Hill to reach a crossroads opposite the ´Whip Inn` at Lacey Green.

Lacey Green - Great Hampden (Map 15)

Maps
OS Landranger Sheet 165
OS Explorer Sheet 181 (or old Sheet 2)
OS Pathfinder Sheet 1118 (SP80/90)
Chiltern Society FP Maps Nos. 7 & 12

Parking
Limited on-street parking is available at Lacey Green.

Lacey Green, stretching along three-quarters of a mile of ridge-top above the Saunderton valley, was till the early twentieth century a hilltop hamlet of Princes Risborough, but the new parish, which had had its own church since 1822, has since expanded through pre-war ribbon development and post-war ´in-filling` into a sizeable village. Its windmill, the oldest surviving smock mill in the country, was originally built at Chesham in 1650, but was dismantled and rebuilt on its present site in 1821. After becoming disused in 1920, the mill became very dilapidated but was painstakingly restored to working order in the 1970s and 1980s by Chiltern Society volunteers.

At the crossroads by the ´Whip Inn`, turn right into Main Road, then immediately left over a stile by a bus shelter onto path L19, following a left-hand hedge through three fields passing Lacey Green Windmill to your left. Where the hedge turns left in the third field, leave it and go straight on across the field to cross a stile under an oak tree, then bear half right across the next field to cross a stile in the far corner. Now take a fenced track straight on to a gate and stile into a field. Here follow the left-hand fence at first, then, where a hedge begins, leave it and go straight on across the field to cross a stile in its far hedge. Now bear half right across the next field to cross a stile into a belt of trees sheltering Grim´s Ditch, an ancient earthwork of unknown origin believed, however, to date from before the Saxon period as ´Grim` is an alternative name for the Germanic god, Wodan, and they are unlikely to have attributed something to a god which they had built themselves. In the trees turn left onto bridleway L21, following Grim´s Ditch to reach a road in Lily Bottom, where the ´Pink & Lily` pub, made famous by the poet Rupert Brooke, who frequented it before the First World War, is a third of a mile to your left.
Turn left onto this road, then immediately right onto bridleway

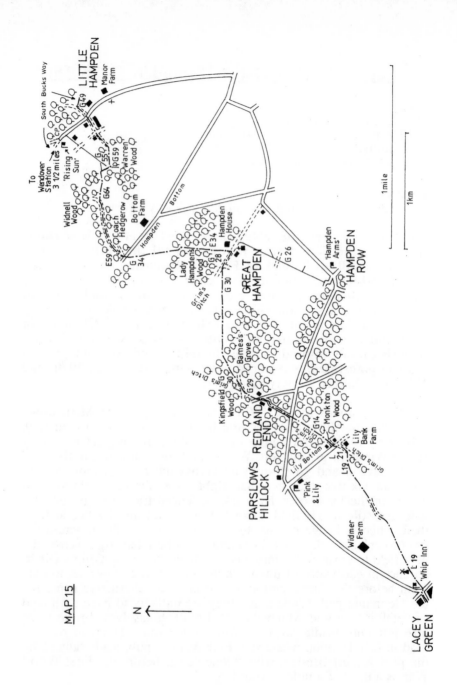

MAP 15

N ←

LITTLE HAMPDEN

Manor Farm

South Bucks Way

G49

To Wendover Station 3 1/2 miles

'Rising Sun'

G 55

G59

G64

Widnell Wood

Coach Hedgerow

Warren Wood

Bottom Farm

E59

G 34

Hampden Bottom

Lady Hampden Wood

Grim's Ditch

E34

Hampden House

G 28

G 30

GREAT HAMPDEN

Hampden Arms'

G 26

HAMPDEN ROW

Kingsfield Wood

G30

Barness Grove

G29

Grim's Ditch

REDLANDS END

PARSLOW'S HILLOCK

Grim's Ditch

G14

Monkton Wood

Lily Bottom

Lily Bank Farm

L 21

Grim's Ditch

'Pink & Lily'

L19

Widmer Farm

L 19

'Whip Inn'

LACEY GREEN

1 mile

1 km

88

G14, following a cottage drive at first, then keeping straight on into Monkton Wood. At two forks take the left-hand option straight on, then go through a fence gap and continue through a plantation, soon passing under a powerline, then bearing left and following the edge of a mature beechwood to a bridlegate and stile leading to a road junction. Here cross the major road and take the road to Redland End and Whiteleaf straight on through the tiny woodland hamlet of Redland End to reach a T-junction.

Here turn left, then, after about 20 yards, turn right over a stile onto path G29, following the bank of Grim's Ditch again through Kingsfield Wood until you reach a crossing track. Now bear right, following waymarks to a waymarked fork where you take the right-hand option (path G30) along a grassy track through Barnes's Grove. At a further fork, keep left and follow a right-hand fence to a stile leading into a large parkland field. Now bear half right across the field, passing right of a tall lightning-damaged tree and through the middle of a large clump of trees, then keep straight on to the far corner of the field. Here cross a stone track and bear slightly right through gates onto bridleway G28, rejoining the course of Grim's Ditch with Hampden House coming into view ahead and follow this wide fenced track to a second set of gates at Great Hampden.

Great Hampden - Little Hampden (Map 15)

Maps
OS Landranger Sheet 165
OS Explorer Sheet 181 (or old Sheet 2)
OS Pathfinder Sheet 1118 (SP80/90)
Chiltern Society FP Maps Nos. 3 & 12

Parking
Limited parking is available where the Way crosses the road in Hampden Bottom.

Great Hampden is typical of many estate villages in having a church and manor house surrounded by a park and its village, called Hampden Row half a mile away on the edge of Hampden Common. Great Hampden was held by the Hampden family (later the Earls of Buckinghamshire) from before the Norman conquest, but the last Earl left Hampden House during the Second World War. The most famous Hampden was John Hampden

(1594 - 1643), the leading Parliamentarian and soldier and cousin of Oliver Cromwell, whose refusal to pay Ship Money in 1635 led to a writ being served upon him at Hampden House and this was one of the significant events leading to the Civil War. The battlemented fourteenth-century house was considerably altered both by John Hampden and again in the eighteenth century and has ceilings and fireplaces by Adam, while the thirteenth-century church, 120 yards ahead to your right, where John Hampden was buried in an unmarked grave after being mortally wounded at Chalgrove Field, contains various monuments to the Hampden family including one erected to John Hampden in 1743.

Just before the gates, turn left over a stile by double gates onto path G34, bearing slightly left across a field past the front of Hampden House to cross a stile into Lady Hampden´s Wood. Now take a wide fenced path downhill through the wood to a gate and stile where fine views open out across Hampden Bottom, home of the late actor and country-lover, Sir Bernard Miles. Now go straight on to the far corner of the field where two tree belts meet. Here cross a stile by gates, the busy road and a stile by gates opposite into a tree belt called Coach Hedgerow noted for its bluebells and take path E59, following the left-hand of two timber tracks gently uphill through the tree belt ignoring all branching tracks. At the far end of the tree belt, where the track bears left into Widnell Wood, turn right onto a crossing track, leaving the wood. Now take path G64 bearing slightly right across the field to a gap in the top hedge, then go straight on uphill through a plantation. On emerging into a field, turn right onto a permissive path kindly provided by the landowner and Chiltern Society President, Sir Leonard Figg, following the edge of the plantation to a corner of the field, then turning left. After 30 yards, turn right onto path G55 into Warren Wood. Having crossed two boundary banks, turn left onto path G59, which leads you to a corner of the wood, then widens into a green lane. On reaching a crossways, take a rough lane straight on to reach a green and the village street at Little Hampden, where you join the South Bucks Way and the ´Rising Sun` is 350 yards to your left.

Here, if wishing to leave the Way for Wendover Station, turn left onto the South Bucks Way and follow it for nearly a mile to reach the Ridgeway, then turn right onto this and follow it for a further two and a half miles to reach the station.

Little Hampden - Lee Gate (Map 16)

Maps
OS Landranger Sheet 165
OS Explorer Sheet 181 (or old Sheet 2)
OS Pathfinder Sheet 1118 (SP80/90)
Chiltern Society FP Map No.3

Parking
There is a small car park on common land at Little Hampden opposite the 'Rising Sun' and a picnic area car park near the Way in Cockshoots Wood. There are also small laybys on the A413 at Wendover Dean.

Little Hampden, on a high ridge at the end of a long winding cul-de-sac lane, has often, with justification, been described as the remotest village in the Buckinghamshire Chilterns. For all this, an extensive network of inviting footpaths radiates from it. This tiny village with its small, rustic thirteenth-century church with its unusual two-storey fifteenth-century porch as well as thirteenth- and fifteenth-century murals, its picturesque old, but recently extended village pub and few farms and cottages was, till 1885, a separate parish. Since then, however, it has been merged with Great Hampden on the other side of Hampden Bottom to form the modern parish of Great and Little Hampden.

Joining the South Bucks Way, cross the road and take path G49 virtually opposite, following a grassy track to a gate and stile into woodland on Little Hampden Common. In the wood, take the track straight on downhill, then, at a fork, bear right onto a waymarked path continuing downhill. On emerging into a field, bear left and follow a right-hand hedge downhill into the valley bottom, where you transfer to the other side of the hedge and continue uphill to a field corner. Here cross a stile into Hampdenleaf Wood, where you keep right at a fork and take the waymarked path steeply uphill, ignoring a crossing path near the top and continuing uphill to a stile into a field. Bear half right across this field to cross two stiles right of a building with a steep roof and a rooflight, then take bridleway G46, bearing slightly right and following a rough lane to Cobblershill Lane in the hilltop hamlet of Cobblers Hill.

Cross this road and take bridleway W45 straight on. Just past a much-extended cottage to your right, leaving the South Bucks Way, turn left onto path W31b entering Cockshoots Wood. In the wood,

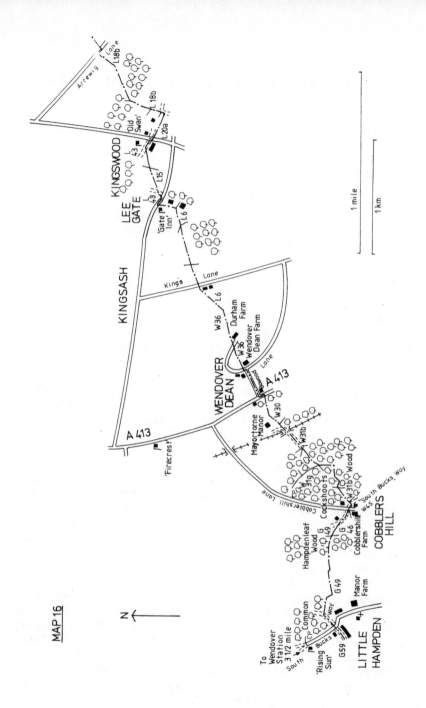

MAP 16

N ←

1 mile

1 km

Arrewig Lane

KINGSWOOD

'Old Swan'

L 18b

L 18b

20a

43

L 15

LEE GATE

L 43

'Gate Inn'

L 6

KINGSASH

Kings Lane

L 6

W 36 Durham Farm

W 36 Wendover Dean Farm

WENDOVER DEAN

'Firecrest'

A 413

A 413

Boswood Lane

W 30

Mayortorne Manor

W 31b

Cobblershill Lane

W 31g

Cockshoots

W 31b Wood

South Bucks Way

W 45

COBBLERS HILL

Hampdenleaf Wood

G 49

G 49

Cobblershill Farm

G 46

G 49

Manor Farm

To Wendover Station 3 1/2 mile

Cop Common

South Bucks Way

'Rising Sun'

G 59

LITTLE HAMPDEN

92

keep left at a fork, following the left-hand edge of a large clearing, then bear slightly right through mature woodland. On reaching a crossing bridleway, bear half right, soon approaching a right-hand field, then follow the inside edge of the wood gently downhill. By a corner of the field, keep left at a fork, then, at a crossways, turn right onto a crossing track, bearing slightly left down a sunken way, eventually reaching the bottom edge of the wood. Here ignore a crossing path and go straight on between posts into a green lane which continues downhill. Where this becomes a stone track, keep straight on (now on path W30), crossing a bridge over a railway, now part of the Chiltern Line, but originally built in 1892 as part of the Metropolitan Railway. Now, where the track turns left, leave it and go straight on through a gate and over a stile into a parkland field. Here go straight on, diverging from the left-hand fence, but keeping just left of the parkland trees and passing Mayortorne Manor to your left, a late eighteenth-century house which, at one time, was home to the noted Chiltern writer, H.J. Massingham. Now cross a stile by a white gate and bear slightly right across the next field, passing between a tall lime tree and a smaller oak to cross a stile into a belt of trees, then a second stile leading to the A413 at Wendover Dean, so called as the manor was once held by the Dean of Wendover.

Turn left onto this road, then, at a road junction, turn right into Bowood Lane and follow it for 300 yards to another junction by Wendover Dean Farm. Here bear slightly left onto path W36, passing through an antique shop car park and crossing a stile by a gate, then go straight on up a field to cross a stile by a tall ash tree. Now cross the narrow lane to Durham Farm and a stile opposite and go straight on through a farm storage area and across a field to a gate and stile in the far hedge. Here bear slightly right up the next field to cross a stile in its top hedge, then take path L6, bearing half left up a field, heading just left of a long white cottage on the skyline when this comes into view to near the left-hand corner of its garage, where you go straight on across a lawn to a garden gate into King's Lane.

Cross this road and a stile opposite and take path L6 straight on to a hedge gap right of a line of trees in the next hedge. Here bear slightly right across the next field, following what is normally a grass crop break to a white marker post right of a lightning-damaged tree, where you keep straight on to cross a stile in the far corner of the field. Now turn left and follow a left-hand hedge past derelict farm buildings, then join a drive and continue through the car park of the 'Gate Inn` to reach a road at Lee Gate.

Lee Gate - Arrewig Lane (Map 16)

Maps
OS Landranger Sheet 165
OS Explorer Sheet 181 (or old Sheet 2)
OS Pathfinder Sheet 1118 (SP80/90)
Chiltern Society FP Map No.8

Parking
There is very limited parking space on or around this section. Do **not** use the ´Gate Inn` car park without the landlord´s permission.

Lee Gate is one of several upland hamlets forming the parish of The Lee. The name Lee derives from the Saxon ´leah` meaning clearing and it is thought that this is the origin of at least the village called The Lee, three-quarters of a mile south of Lee Gate, where the original thirteenth-century church, its replacement built in 1868 and Church Farm stand within an ancient camp, a circular earthwork, where there is also evidence of a deserted village, and there is a picturesque village green surrounded by a pub, a manor house, a farm and old cottages which is frequently used as a film set. Other hamlets are frequently named after local features; in Lee Gate´s case, the inn which forms its focal point.

By the ´Gate Inn` turn right onto the road. After 70 yards, fork left into Furze Field Lane (L43). At a left-hand bend, leave it and take path L15 straight on through a hedge gap and across a field, heading just left of several cottages ahead to pass through a gap in the next hedge. Now bear half left across the next field to a hedge gap in the far corner left of the cottages. Here rejoin L43 and take this rough road to reach a road by the ´Old Swan` at Kingswood.
   Turn right onto this road, passing Jim´s Seat, then turn left over a concealed stile by a gate onto path L20a, following a wide fenced grass strip. Where this widens to your left, follow the right-hand side of a line of trees straight on to cross a stile into a green lane. Now turn left, crossing a stile in metal rails ahead and taking path L18b beside a left-hand hedge through two fields, ignoring the stile of a branching path to your left. At the far end of the second field, cross a stile into a strip of woodland, then fork right crossing the wood diagonally. On leaving the wood, keep straight on over a rise to the point where three hedges meet in the next dip. Here go through a hedge gap and take the right-hand side of a hedge straight on uphill to a hedge gap leading to Arrewig Lane.

Arrewig Lane - St. Leonard's (Map 17)

Maps
OS Landranger Sheet 165
OS Explorer Sheet 181 (or old Sheet 2)
OS Pathfinder Sheet 1118 (SP80/90)
Chiltern Society FP Map No.8

Parking
There is very limited parking space on or around this section.

The unusual names of Arrewig Lane and nearby Erriwig Farm are often thought to be rustic corruptions of ´earwig`, but, in fact, they are more likely to be of Saxon origin and to derive from the lane, (which probably dates from Saxon times as it follows the ancient parish boundary between the hillfoot strip parishes of Wendover and Aston Clinton and since 1932 between The Lee and Cholesbury-cum-St. Leonards), leading to traditionally arable fields and it thus means ´way to the arable fields`.

Turn right into Arrewig Lane, then, after 50 yards, turn left through a hedge gap onto path CY46, heading for the left-hand side of a clump of trees surrounding a pond. Now bear slightly right across the field to a hedge gap into a wood called Lady Grove. In the wood, ignore a crossing path and bear slightly left, soon going uphill to pass between a green shed and a pond, then bearing left to reach another field. Go straight on across this field to enter the right-hand end of a wood called Ashen Grove where you soon reach crossing bridleway CY6, an ancient road called Broad Street Lane. Turn right onto this, leaving the wood and continuing along a green lane, eventually reaching a bend in a concrete farm road. Take this straight on, passing the moated Dundridge Manor to your right. There is thought to have been a manor house on this site since Saxon times and its name, which was documented in the thirteenth century as ´Dunrugge`, derives from the Saxon ´Dun-hrycg` meaning ´bare ridge`, but habitation of the area dates back even further as Iron Age pottery has been found here.

On passing some gates, you will see the drawbridge to your right. Now go straight on along a fine avenue of mature beech trees, keeping left at a fork to reach Oak Lane. Turn left onto this road, then, at a road junction, turn left again into Jenkins Lane and follow it for 100 yards to a left-hand bend by the ´White Lion` at St. Leonard's.

MAP 17

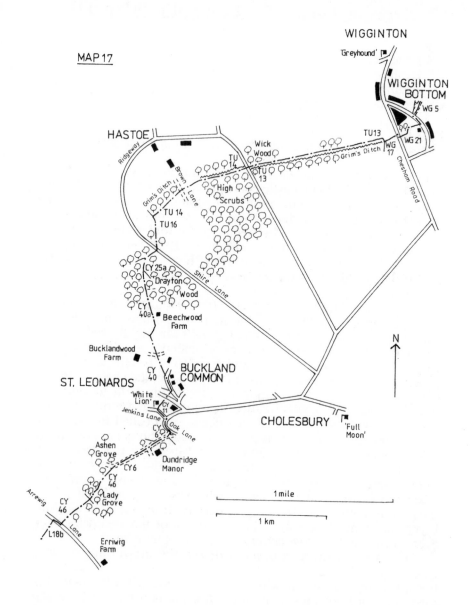

WIGGINTON

'Greyhound'

WIGGINTON BOTTOM

WG 5

HASTOE

Ridgeway

Brown Lane

Grim's Ditch

Wick Wood

TU

TU 13

Grim's Ditch

WG 17

WG 21

TU13

Chesham Road

High Scrubs

TU 14

TU 16

Shire Lane

CY 25a

Drayton Wood

CY 40a

Beechwood Farm

N

Bucklandwood Farm

CY 40

BUCKLAND COMMON

ST. LEONARDS

'White Lion'

CY 11

Jenkins Lane

Oak Lane

CHOLESBURY

'Full Moon'

CY 6

Ashen Grove

Dundridge Manor

CY 6

CY 46

Arrewig

CY 46

Lady Grove

Lane

1 mile

1 km

L18b

Erriwig Farm

96

St. Leonard's - Buckland Common (Map 17)

Maps
OS Landranger Sheet 165
OS Explorer Sheet 181 (or old Sheet 2)
OS Pathfinder Sheet 1118 (SP80/90)
Chiltern Society FP Map No.8

Parking
There is very limited parking space on or around this section. Do not use the 'White Lion' car park without the landlord's permission.

St. Leonard's, a scattered, remote Chiltern hamlet some 700 feet above sea level, was, till 1932, an upland hamlet of the seven-mile-long strip parish of Aston Clinton. Despite this, however, due to its remoteness from the mother church nearly four miles away at the foot of the escarpment, St. Leonard's has had its own chapel-of-ease since at least the thirteenth century and the present picturesque building dates from the fifteenth century.

On reaching the 'White Lion', turn right onto path CY11, passing through the pub car park and crossing a stile by a gate, then go straight on downhill, passing right of two clumps of bushes to cross a stile by a gate into Bottom Road. Now cross a stile by a gate opposite and bear half right across the next field to cross a stile by a gate onto Little Twye Road at Buckland Common.

Buckland Common - Wigginton (Map 17)

Maps
OS Landranger Sheet 165
OS Explorer Sheet 181 (or old Sheet 2)
OS Pathfinder Sheet 1118 (SP80/90)
Chiltern Society FP Map No.8

Parking
There is limited parking space on verges at Buckland Common.

Until 1932, Buckland Common was another upland hamlet of a hillfoot strip parish, in this case, as its name suggests, Buckland, but this settlement is thought to be more recent and an example of unauthorised encroachment on a remote common.

Turn left onto Little Twye Road, passing a large white cottage, the former ´Boot & Slipper` pub. At a right-hand bend, fork left over a stile by a gate onto path CY40, bearing half right across a field towards a group of trees left of a garden shed, to reach a gap in the far hedge leading to a farm road. Cross this road and a stile opposite, then follow a right-hand hedge to cross a stile in the far corner of the field. Now turn right onto path CY40a, following a right-hand hedge through two fields to cross a stile into Drayton Wood, whose name reminds us that this wood was formerly part of yet another hillfoot strip parish, Drayton Beauchamp, which till mediæval times, also included Cholesbury. In the wood, follow an obvious winding path generally straight on. At a waymarked junction, take path CY25a, bearing slightly left and keeping right at a further waymarked junction to reach a gate and stile into a field. Here go straight on across the field to cross a stile into Shire Lane, so called as it marks the ancient county boundary between Buckinghamshire and Hertfordshire.

Now in Hertfordshire, cross a stile opposite into a strip of woodland and take path TU16, bearing half left through the trees to enter a field. Here bear half left across the field to the corner of a hedge, then bear half left again and follow the hedge to a field corner. Now turn right onto path TU14, following the outside edge of a tree belt shading another section of Grim´s Ditch, an ancient earthwork of unknown origin believed, however, to date from before the Saxon period as ´Grim` is an alternative name for the Germanic god, Wodan, and they are unlikely to have attributed something to a god which they had built themselves. At the far end of the tree belt, go straight on through a hedge gap into Brown´s Lane, an ancient green lane, where Hastoe, at 770 feet the highest village in Hertfordshire (no pub) and the Ridgeway are a third of a mile to your left.

Here take path TU14 straight on through a hedge gap opposite and continue to a corner of a wood called High Scrubs. Now enter the wood and keep straight on for over a quarter mile, following another surviving section of Grim´s Ditch and eventually crossing a stile by a gate onto a road. Cross this road and take path TU13 straight on over a stile opposite, following Grim´s Ditch through Wick Wood, then generally along the edge of a tree belt. Where the trees peter out, take a grassy track straight on until you reach a hedge, then turn right and follow it for 35 yards. Now turn left over a stile onto path WG17 and go straight across a field to a stile onto Chesham Road on the edge of Wigginton, where the ´Greyhound` is a third of a mile to your left.

Wigginton - Aldbury (Map 18)

Maps
OS Landranger Sheet 165
OS Explorer Sheet 181 (or old Sheet 2)
OS Pathfinder Sheets 1094 (SP81/91) & 1118 (SP80/90)
Chiltern Society FP Maps Nos. 8 or 18 & 19

Parking
On-street parking is possible at Wigginton and there is a small car park on Tom's Hill Road east of Aldbury.

Wigginton, a hilltop Chiltern village above Tring with superb views in places across the surrounding countryside, was, at one time, very much an estate village housing workers from Lord Rothschild's estate at Tring Park and many of its sturdy nineteenth-century cottages were, indeed, originally built by this benevolent estate. Just to the south is the well-known health farm of Champneys in a house which also dates from this period, while the mediæval parish church was largely rebuilt in 1881, but retains the fifteenth-century West Chamber. Like many other villages in the northern Chilterns, Wigginton was, in the nineteenth century, also a centre for straw-plaiting which supplied the hat-making industry of Luton and Dunstable.

Turn right into Chesham Road. After 20 yards, turn left through a hedge gap onto path WG21 through a copse then between a hedge and a fence, eventually reaching a road at Wigginton Bottom. Turn left onto this road, then in the bottom of a dip, turn right onto path WG5, following a short lane into a field, then taking a grassy track uphill beside a right-hand hedge. Where the track leaves the hedge and becomes less distinct, keep straight on to rejoin the right-hand hedge by some ash trees. Now follow it, bearing right to enter a green lane, along which you continue until you enter Lower Wood. Here keep right at a fork and take path WG6 generally straight on through the wood, eventually dropping into a valley bottom. At a T-junction turn right onto path WG8, soon leaving the wood by a stile and following a left-hand fence straight on to a stile at the far end of the field. Now go straight on across the next field to a stile into a green lane (path WG11). Turn right into this lane, which soon becomes a concrete road and bears right beside the A41 Berkhamsted Bypass, then descends to reach Bottom House Lane.
　　Turn left onto this road, passing under the A41 bridge, then, by

a large house called Tinker's Lodge, turn right onto byway WG10, following its drive at first, then continuing along a rough lane. After this bears left, ignore a branching path to your right and keep straight on for a third of a mile, joining a rough macadam road and eventually reaching the A4251 at Cow Roast by the 'Cow Roast Inn'. The inn, after which the hamlet is named, is thought originally to have been called the 'Cow Rest' and to have been a resting place for cattle drovers on their way along the main road to London.

Turn right onto the A4251, then, just past the inn, turn left onto a narrow road, crossing a bridge over the Grand Union Canal by Cow Roast Lock. Here, if wishing to leave the Way for Tring Station, turn left down a ramp onto the towpath and follow it for 1.4 miles to the second crossing road bridge where the station is to your right. Otherwise, continue along the lane, bearing right, then after 150 yards, turn left over a concealed stile onto path NC29, bearing slightly right across a field to cross a high footbridge over the former L&NWR Euston-Birmingham main line built in 1838, the height of which was raised when what is now known as the West Coast main line was electrified in the 1960s. Now keep straight on across the next field to pass through a hedge gap. Here turn right onto a fenced grassy track, then, at a T-junction, turn left (still on path NC29), soon crossing a stile by a gate and bearing slightly right to reach the drive to Norcott Court Farm.

Turn sharp left onto this, crossing a stile by a gate, then turn right over another stile by a gate into a field. Here bear half left, crossing the field diagonally with fine views across the Tring Gap in the Chiltern escarpment to your left including the spectacular sloping footbridge carrying the Ridgeway over the A41. At the far corner of the field, cross a stile by a gate and go straight on across the next field to the corner of a hedge. Keep left of this hedge and follow it to a field corner. Here bear half right through the thick hedge and up a bank to cross a stile, then take path AB3, bearing half left over a rise to cross a stile in the far corner of the field. Now follow the edge of a wood called The Hangings for 50 yards, looking out for a gate into it. Turn right through this onto byway AB1, taking a track gently uphill through the wood. After passing through a series of gates, take a stony track straight on past an industrial site to a gate leading to a macadam road at Tom's Hill.

Follow this straight on, keeping left by Rose Cottage and then ignoring branching paths to left and right. On reaching a T-junction at a hairpin bend in Tom's Hill Road, fork left onto the major road. Where its left-hand crash-barrier ends, fork left again onto path AB39, taking a terraced woodland path steeply downhill to reach the end of a village street in Aldbury called Malting Lane.

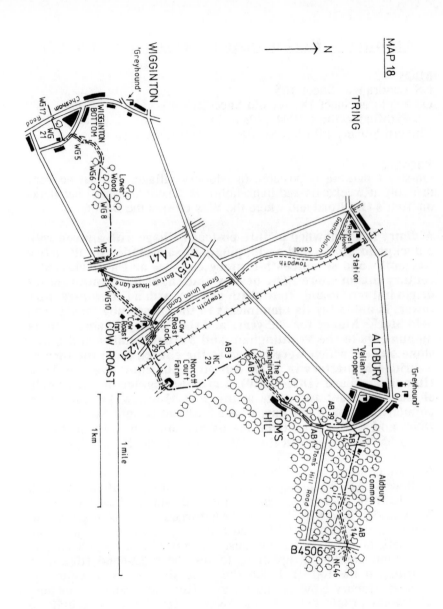

Aldbury - Berkhamsted Common (Map 18)

Maps
OS Landranger Sheet 165
OS Explorer Sheet 181 (or old Sheet 2)
OS Pathfinder Sheet 1094 (SP81/91)
Chiltern Society FP Map No.19

Parking
On-street parking is possible in Aldbury village, but can be very difficult at weekends and bank holidays. There are small car parks on Tom's Hill Road and where the Way crosses the B4506.

Aldbury is a renowned picture-postcard village with a green with a duckpond, stocks and a whipping-post surrounded by attractive sixteenth- and seventeenth-century cottages and a seventeenth-century manor house. The nearby church, of thirteenth-century origin but now mainly fourteenth-century with a fifteenth-century tower, is noted for its monuments to the Duncombe family who held Stocks Manor for 500 years and the Pendley Chapel with its monuments to the Whittingham and Verney families and a fine stone screen, which were moved to the church from the former Ashridge Monastery in 1575. Buried in the churchyard is Mrs. Humphrey Ward (1851 -1920), a grand-daughter of Dr. Arnold of Rugby School and niece of the poet Matthew Arnold and a popular novelist of her day, whose husband bought Stocks in the 1890s and who was visited there by her son-in-law, the historian Dr. G.M. Trevelyan and the playwright George Bernard Shaw.

Do not continue into Malting Lane, but turn sharp right onto bridleway AB14, taking a sunken way steeply uphill through woodland on Aldbury Common, much of which, since the sale of the Ashridge Estate in 1929, has been owned by the National Trust. You soon cross Tom's Hill Road and then, at a five-way junction, bear half left up a steep slope. Just past a dead tree covered in ivy, fork right, continuing uphill to follow the right-hand edge of a clearing, at the top of which there are fine views to your left towards Aldbury Nowers and Pitstone Hill. Now ignore branching bridleways to left and right and keep straight on, passing under a powerline, soon crossing a drive by a lodge and taking the main track straight on for half a mile, ignoring all branching or crossing paths or tracks to cross the B4506 by a corner of a field to your left onto Berkhamsted Common.

Berkhamsted Common - Little Gaddesden (Map 19)

Maps
OS Landranger Sheet 165
OS Explorer Sheet 181 (or old Sheet 2)
OS Pathfinder Sheet 1094 (SP81/91)
Chiltern Society FP Map No.19

Parking
There is a small car park where the Way crosses the B4506.

Berkhamsted Common with its extensive woodland is today taken for granted as a place where local people and Londoners can go for fresh air and exercise, but few of its many visitors realise that in 1866 it was all but lost to land enclosure. In that year, 400 acres of the Common, which had, in mediæval times, formed part of the park of Berkhamsted's Norman castle, were enclosed by the lord of the manor, Lord Brownlow of Ashridge Park with a high iron fence. This might easily have led to the land being split into fields and brought into agricultural use, but Augustus Smith, owner of the nearby Ashlyns Estate and one of the enraged Berkhamsted commoners, supported by Lord Eversley, chairman of the newly-founded Commons Preservation Society (now renamed as the Open Spaces Society), assembled a gang of 100 London labourers and chartered a special train to bring them by dead of night to Berkhamsted Common. By 6 a.m. the fence had been completely dismantled and four years of litigation followed, but finally in 1870 Augustus Smith won with an injunction being granted forbidding enclosure and defining the rights of common. This judgment did not, of course, give public access but preserved the rights of common, so that, when the Law of Property Act 1925 granted public access to urban commons, Berkhamsted Common was able to qualify, subject to certain limitations to protect the golf course.

From the B4506, take bridleway NC46 straight on eastwards for a quarter mile along an avenue of ancient beech and oak trees with a pronounced boundary bank to your left. By the corner of a field to your left, turn left onto path LG5, following the inside edge of the wood. Where the field fence turns away to your right, go straight on, soon wiggling to your right, passing right of a pond and joining a track which merges from your left. On reaching a bend in a macadam private road, join it and follow it straight on, soon crossing a grassy avenue called Prince's Riding, where Ashridge House can be seen two thirds of a mile to your right and the Bridgewater Monument is nearly a mile to your left.

Ashridge House, which has been variously described as being 'like a snowman, built up by sticking on lumps instead of having good bones inside it' and by the Chiltern writer, H.J. Massingham as being 'like a gigantic wedding cake' and 'hideous but ... also comic', was commissioned by the third Duke of Bridgewater before his death in 1803 to replace a mediæval house, which had passed to his family in 1604 and had formerly been a monastery. Designed in the neo-Gothic style by James Wyatt and his nephew, Sir Jeffry Wyatville, it was eventually completed in about 1820. At the other end of the Riding, which forms part of the landscaping carried out by Capability Brown in about 1767, is the Bridgewater Monument, a tall Doric column also designed by Sir Jeffry Wyatville and erected in 1832 in memory of the third Duke, who is noted as 'the Father of British Inland Navigation'.

On emerging from the woods onto Ashridge Golf Course, keep straight on past Old Park Lodge, where the macadam surface gives way to stone, to reach an old farmyard. Here, by an oak tree, bear half right onto a wide track downhill through the wood, keeping left at a fork to emerge onto another part of the golf course. Now bear slightly right, passing right of a green and left of the clubhouse, then follow the outside edge of a wood straight on. Where a macadam drive approaches from your right by the corner of a chain-link fence, join the drive and follow it straight on to a T-junction. Here, leaving the drive, bear half right through the trees, crossing another drive and taking a fenced track (still path LG5) straight on between gardens into woodland. On reemerging onto the golf course, ignore a crossing golfers' path and go straight on downhill between tees and through woodland to the bottom of a dip known as Witchcraft Bottom. Here take a fenced path straight on between gardens, soon crossing a drive and continuing uphill to a private road. Cross this and take the fenced path straight on uphill to a stile into the 'Bridgewater Arms' car park and the road through Little Gaddesden.

Little Gaddesden - Studham (Map 19)

Maps
OS Landranger Sheets 165 & 166
OS Explorer Sheet 181
OS Pathfinder Sheets 1094 (SP81/91) & 1095 (TL01/11)
Chiltern Society FP Maps Nos. 19 & 20

Parking
There is a small car park in Church Road, Little Gaddesden. Do **not** use the ´Bridgewater Arms` car park without the landlord´s permission.

Little Gaddesden, a long straggling village, most of which is on one side of the Ringshall - Nettleden road with Ashridge Park on the other, can boast an attractive village green by which is a timber-framed cottage with an overhanging upper floor called John o´Gaddesden´s House, which was reputedly home to this fourteenth-century doctor to Edward II and Edward III, who died in 1361, but is thought more likely to date from the fifteenth century. The stone-built manor house also dates from 1576, while the fifteenth-century parish church, which stands in splendid isolation in fields at the end of a cul-de-sac lane, is principally notable for the wealth of memorials it contains to members of the Egerton family, the Earls and Dukes of Bridgewater, who held nearby Ashridge from 1604 to 1849.

Turn right onto the road, then, after 50 yards, turn left through a kissing-gate onto path LG12, following a fenced path between paddocks, glimpsing the church through a gap in the trees ahead and ignoring a branching path to your right. Having passed through two more gates, you emerge into a meadow where you bear slightly right, passing the corner of a fenced garden to reach a stile in the far corner of the field leading to Church Lane. Turn left onto this road, then immediately right over a stile and bear half left across a paddock with fine views of the church to your left. Having crossed another stile, bear half left across the next field to cross the left-hand of two stiles in the next fence. Now bear half left again across a prairie field, heading for a large oak tree some way left of a distant cottage, eventually passing the oak tree to reach the far corner of the field. Here ignore a stile on a crossing path and bear half left through a hedge gap, following a right-hand hedge downhill with fine views opening out across the Gade valley ahead, eventually passing a copse and reaching a gap in the bottom hedge. Now ignore a bridlegate to your right and join bridleway LG11, following a grassy track straight on downhill beside a right-hand hedge, soon crossing the Bedfordshire boundary and continuing (now on bridleway ST33) to the A4146 in the valley bottom.

Cross this road and take bridleway ST25 straight on, passing through a gap left of a padlocked gate and following a left-hand hedge uphill. Soon after the hedge bears right, pass through a hedge gap, where there is a fine view to your left towards Ivinghoe Beacon, then go straight on uphill between a hedge and a deer fence protecting a young plantation, passing a copse to your right and eventually reaching a gate into Ravensdell Wood. Keep straight on through this wood to a gate into a field, then follow a grassy track beside a right-hand hedge straight on. After 50 yards, turn right over a stile onto path ST26 and bear half left across a field, aiming just left of a line of three trees and a cottage with white window frames at Studham beyond and eventually crossing a stile. Now go straight on, passing left of a lightning-damaged ash tree to cross a stile by a gate left of the cottage, then follow a short drive to a gate and stile onto Common Road on the edge of Studham.

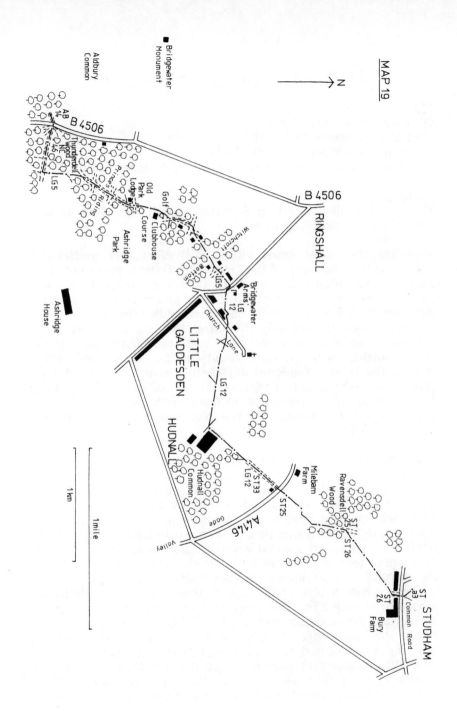

MAP 19

→ N

Bridgewater
Monument ■

Aldbury
Common

B 4506

AB
14

Thunderdell
Wood NC6

LG6

LG5

Princes Riding

Old
Park
Lodge

Ashridge
Park

Golf
Course

Clubhouse

B 4506

RINGSHALL

Witchcraft
Bottom

LG5

Bridgewater
Arms'
LG
12

Church

LG

Lane

†

LITTLE
GADDESDEN

Ashridge
House

LG 12

HUDNALL

Hudnall
Common

LG12

ST33

ST25

Milebarn
Farm

A4146

Gade
Valley

Ravensdell
Wood

ST
35

ST 26

1 km

1 mile

STUDHAM

ST
26

ST
33

Common
Road

Bury
Farm

107

Studham - Whipsnade (Map 20)

Maps
OS Landranger Sheet 166
OS Explorer Sheets 181 or 182
OS Pathfinder Sheet 1095 (TL01/11)
Chiltern Society FP Maps Nos. 20 & 21 (to be published in 2001)

Parking
There is a small car park at Studham Church, but avoid using it when there are church services.

Studham, the southernmost village in Bedfordshire, nestles in a hollow in the backland of the Dunstable Downs, surrounded by an extensive upland plateau. Until 1897, the village, which was once a centre of the straw-plait industry and was one of the early strongholds of Nonconformity, in fact straddled the Hertfordshire boundary and it was only then that the southern half of its extensive common and many of its scattered farms and cottages were transferred to the same county as the church and village centre. The cement-rendered thirteenth-century church, which is somewhat isolated and hidden at the end of its cul-de-sac lane, has a surprisingly beautiful interior with fine carved stone capitals and an unusual carved Norman font predating the present building.

Bear slightly right across Common Road and go through a hedge gap, then bear half left onto path STa3, heading for the bottom left-hand corner of the field. Here go through a hedge gap, cross Valley Road and take path ST23 through another gap opposite, following the right-hand hedge through two fields. In the second field turn right over a stile by a gate onto path ST20, going straight uphill to a corner of a wood called Castle Grove, then follow its edge uphill to a stile leading to bridleway ST6 (where the road to the church is a short distance to your right).

Here ignore a blue-green gate to your left and turn left onto fenced bridleway ST6, soon entering a wood called Church Grove. Just inside the wood, disregard a branching path to your left and follow the inside edge of the wood straight on for a quarter mile, ignoring a signposted crossing path and two branching paths to your left. On emerging from the wood into a field corner, ignore a branching track to your right and take a grassy track beside a right-hand hedge straight on through two fields. At the far end of the second field, go straight on into a copse, then, at a fork, take the right-hand option straight on, joining the Icknield Way long-distance path and soon reaching the perimeter fence of Whipsnade Wild Animal Park. Now keep straight on between this fence and a tree belt for over a quarter mile to reach Studham Lane. Turn left into this narrow road closed to through-traffic and follow it for a quarter mile. Where the lane forks, keep right, then immediately turn right over a stile onto path ST10, leaving the Icknield Way long-distance path and following a left-hand hedge to cross a stile at the far side of the field. Now turn left over a stile by a gate onto path WP8 and follow a right-hand hedge towards Whipsnade Church. At the far side of the field, cross a stile into the churchyard and pass left of the church to reach gates leading out to Whipsnade Green.

Whipsnade - Dunstable Downs (Map 20)

Maps
OS Landranger Sheet 166
OS Explorer Sheets 181 or 182
OS Pathfinder Sheet 1095 (TL01/11)
Chiltern Society FP Map No.21 (to be published in 2001)

Parking
There are car parks at Whipsnade Tree Cathedral and just off the B4540 at Whipsnade Down.

Whipsnade village is notable for the extensive green, around which its scattered cottages are situated, and being the highest village in Bedfordshire. Its unusual brick-built church has a sixteenth-century tower and an eighteenth-century nave but incorporates details of an earlier building, while, at the back of the village, is the Tree Cathedral planted in the 1930s by Edmund Kell Blyth in memory of friends killed in the First World War and now looked after by the National Trust. However what Whipsnade is best known for is the Wild Animal Park, which was opened by the Royal Zoological Society in 1931 to exhibit and breed its hardier animals in natural surroundings. The Wild Animal Park in its scenically spectacular setting can be toured by a steam railway which you may have heard while skirting the Park´s perimeter on bridleway ST6.

At the church gates, turn left and follow the back of the green at first. Having crossed the drive to Church Farm, keep straight on to a road junction left of a former chapel. Here cross the B4540 and take the road signposted to the 'Tree Cathedral'. At a fork, keep right, then immediately bear right again through a gap by a padlocked gate onto bridleway WP4, following a green lane past the Tree Cathedral. On reaching a kissing-gate into the Tree Cathedral to your left, bear right to pass through a fence gap onto a private road.

Turn left onto this road, then, after 70 yards, fork right, following a right-hand hedge through scrubland, part of the Sallow Springs Nature Reserve, then along the edge of a meadow. At the far side of the meadow, follow the hedge straight on into more scrubland, soon turning left and following a right-hand fence to rejoin the private road. Turn right onto this, ignoring a branching path to your left and the entrance to a luxury housing development to your right and soon entering Sallowspring Wood. At the far side of the wood, by a telecommunications mast, fork right, joining bridleway WP1 which follows a green lane along the edge of the wood. On emerging onto another private road, take a sunken way straight on along the edge of the wood to reach a bridlegate leading to Whipsnade Down, where superb panoramic views open out with a glider airfield below you, Dunstable Downs to your right, Totternhoe Knolls ahead and the Vale of Aylesbury beyond. Here turn right onto a National Trust permissive bridleway, following the top hedge of the Down for 250 yards to reach a bridlegate. Go through this, then follow a right-hand fence straight on through scrubland. On emerging onto open downland, go straight on over a slight rise, where a superb view along the Dunstable Downs opens out ahead, to reach the Countryside Centre.

MAP 20

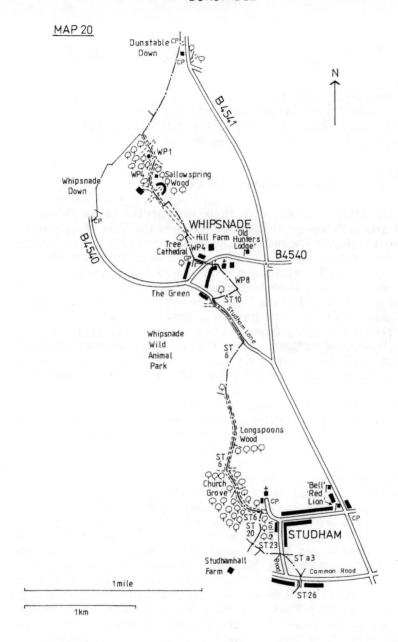

Dunstable Downs - Dunstable (Map 21)

Maps
OS Landranger Sheet 166
OS Explorer Sheets 181 or 182 & 193
OS Pathfinder Sheets 1072 (TL02/12) & 1095 (TL01/11)
Chiltern Society FP Map No.21 (to be published in 2001)

Parking
There are car parks at Dunstable Downs.

The Dunstable Downs, with their spectacular views along the Chilterns to Ivinghoe Beacon and out over the Vale of Aylesbury towards Oxfordshire and the Cotswolds, are today a real 'honey-pot` for people from Dunstable, Luton and farther afield, for picnics and walks with superb views and ample parking. Four thousand years ago these hills must also have been frequented, as, at the northern end of the Downs, are the Five Knolls, five huge Neolithic or Bronze Age barrows, where excavations have not only revealed remains from this period, but also a large number of skeletons originating from the fifth century AD, some of whom had injured bones or their hands tied behind their backs, suggesting that they were the victims of some battle or massacre.

By the Countryside Centre, bear slightly left and pass between wooden posts, then take a chalky track straight on across an overflow car park. By the car park entrance, keep straight on, passing between more wooden posts, now with additional views behind you towards Ivinghoe Beacon, and taking the right-hand of two worn grassy paths straight on parallel to the B4541 to your right. Eventually you pass through a gate and bridlegate right of a kissing-gate and join a chalky path, part of the Icknield Way long-distance path. Follow this, passing the top of a deep steep-sided coombe called Pascomb Pit, with further views briefly opening out to your right across Dunstable, Houghton Regis and Luton with Blows Down to your right. Now at a three-way fork, take the central option to the summit of Five Knolls Hill, where you have panoramic views in all directions. Here bear half right, passing left of four of the Five Knolls and then descending through a kissing-gate and joining path D23 to reach mown parkland at the bottom of the slope. Now follow a right-hand line of trees, bearing left when nearing the B4541 to reach a roundabout on the edge of Dunstable at the junction of the B489 and B4541.

Dunstable - Chalk Hill (Map 21)

Maps
OS Landranger Sheets 165 & 166
OS Explorer Sheets 192 & 193
OS Pathfinder Sheets 1071 (SP82/92) & 1072 (TL02/12)
(part only) Chiltern Society FP Map No.21 (due in 2001)

Parking
On-street parking is possible in residential roads near the Way on
the outskirts of Dunstable.

**Dunstable, the centre of which is three-quarters of a mile to your
right, is situated at the crossroads of the prehistoric Icknield Way
(now the B489) and Watling Street, a Roman road from Dover
via London to Holyhead (now the A5). The area is believed to
have been inhabited since the Stone Age, as archæologists have
made finds dating from various ages in close proximity to the
town. Although a Roman staging post known as Durocobrivæ
was recorded, it is believed not to have been very large and it
was only in 1131, when King Henry I founded an Augustinian
priory and constructed a royal lodge known as Kingsbury, that
'Dunestaple' (as it was then known) became a place of any size.
Originally the Priory was of vast proportions, being 320 feet
long and having transepts 150 feet wide, but the west towers
collapsed in a storm in 1222 and the transepts, central tower,
long choir and monastic buildings were, at some stage,
demolished to leave the present parish church with its massive
Norman columns, round arches and fifteenth-century north
tower. In 1533 the Priory was also the scene of a major historical
event, as it was here that Thomas Cranmer, the then Archbishop
of Canterbury, pronounced the annulment of the marriage of
Henry VIII and Catherine of Aragon, which led to the English
Reformation. In the eighteenth century, improved road
communications caused Dunstable to become an important port
of call for stagecoaches and so the town's inns flourished, as did
the local straw-hat industry, but it has only been in the last
century that Dunstable has mushroomed into the large industrial
town it is today.**

Now cross the B489 (Tring Road) left of the roundabout, passing
the left-hand end of a post-and-rail fence, then bear half right,
passing through a squeeze-stile beside a gate and taking byway D4

along the surprisingly rural, wide, tree-lined Green Lane between housing estates, soon ignoring a crossing macadam path and passing through a former gateway. Now on byway TT12, continue for a further third of a mile, ignoring all branching or crossing paths or tracks, later with fine views through gaps in the left-hand hedge along the Chiltern escarpment including the Dunstable Downs, Whipsnade Down with its white lion cut in the chalk hillside in 1933 as an advertisement for the newly-opened zoo, Ivinghoe Beacon, Aston Hill and more hills beyond. Some 250 yards beyond the end of the right-hand tree belt, where encroaching scrub begins markedly to reduce the usable width of the lane, turn right onto bridleway HR35, following a grassy track beside a left-hand hedge with views ahead towards Houghton Regis with its prominent fifteenth-century church tower. Where the hedge and track bear left, follow them, looking out through gaps in the left-hand hedge for a circular earthwork capped by hedge called Maiden Bower, a large Iron Age plateau-fort built on the site of Neolithic causewayed enclosures. Near this, the track becomes enclosed in a green lane and starts to descend, soon bearing left and following Sewell Cutting to your right, part of the former Dunstable Branch of the London & North Western Railway, closed in 1962, where Roman pottery was found during construction of the railway in 1859 and which is now a nature reserve noted for its chalkland flowers.

At the bottom of the hill, where old chalk quarry faces can be seen to your left and the former railway is now on a low embankment, turn right between old bridge abutments into Sewell Lane. Now follow this road through the picturesque hamlet of Sewell for nearly a quarter mile. Just past the drive to Sewell Manor, turn left through a fence gap onto path HR24 (still on the Icknield Way long-distance path), following a fenced path downhill to cross a stile, then bearing right to cross two more stiles and reach a field. Bear slightly left across this field to cross a stile under a tall sycamore tree, then turn left onto a sometimes overgrown path through a tree belt, eventually emerging over a footbridge into a field. Now turn right and follow this ditch and a sporadic hedge until you reach a tree belt covering the embankment of the A5. Here turn right onto path HR31, following the edge of the tree belt until a marker post indicates a hedge gap leading to a steep flight of steps up the embankment to cross a stile onto the A5 at Chalk Hill.

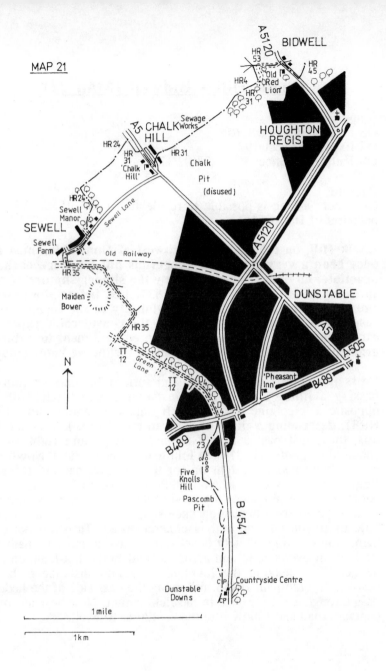

MAP 21

BIDWELL

A5120

HR
53

HR4

'Old
Red
Lion'

HR
45

HR
31

Sewage
Works

HOUGHTON
REGIS

CHALK
HILL

A5

HR 24

HR
31
'Chalk
Hill'

HR 31

Chalk

Pit

(disused)

HR24

Sewell
Manor

Sewell Lane

A5120

SEWELL

Sewell
Farm

Old Railway

DUNSTABLE

HR 35

A5

Maiden
Bower

A505

HR 35

TT
12

Green
Lane

'Pheasant
Inn'

B489

TT
12

D4

B489

D
23

Five
Knolls
Hill

B4541

Pascomb
Pit

N

C/P

Countryside Centre

Dunstable
Downs

C/P

1 mile

1 km

115

Chalk Hill - Bidwell (Map 21)

Maps
OS Landranger Sheet 166
OS Explorer Sheet 193
OS Pathfinder Sheet 1072 (TL02/12)

Parking
On-street parking is possible in residential roads off the A5 on the outskirts of Dunstable.

Chalk Hill, on the A5 just northwest of Dunstable, must have once been a very steep and dangerous hill for stagecoaches to negotiate, no doubt exacerbated by the slippery nature of chalk surfaces in wet weather, as, in 1837, just before the dawning railway age ruined the financial viability of the turnpikes, the responsible turnpike trust went to the considerable expense of excavating a cutting and creating an embankment to reduce its gradient and produce the long gradual incline we know today.

Cross the main road carefully and turn right onto its footway, passing a filling station, then, just before the 'Chalk Hill' inn, opposite a telephone box, turn left onto the continuation of path HR31, descending a flight of steps to the old road. Turn left onto this, then, just past a timber-framed cottage, turn right onto an enclosed path (still HR31) and follow it to enter a field. Now follow its left-hand hedge straight on for half a mile, passing Houghton Regis Sewage Works to your left and eventually reaching the corner of a copse concealing an old chalkpit. Here go straight on, with the path soon becoming enclosed, and continue for a quarter mile until you emerge onto a concrete road. Turn left onto this, then, where it immediately bears right, leave it and take path HR4 straight on over a stile and across a field to the left-hand end of a hedge. Here, leaving the Icknield Way long-distance path, turn sharp right onto path HR53, following the near side of the hedge to pass through a kissing-gate in the field corner. Now bear left onto a concrete road and follow it to the A5120 at Bidwell.

Bidwell - Chalton (Map 22)

Maps
OS Landranger Sheet 166
OS Explorer Sheet 193
OS Pathfinder Sheet 1072 (TL02/12)

Parking
On-street parking is possible in residential roads off the A5120 on
the outskirts of Houghton Regis.

**Bidwell, an attractive hamlet of Houghton Regis at the foot of the
hill on the Bedford road with an inn and half-timbered farm-
houses and cottages, has today almost been swallowed up by its
larger neighbour, which has expanded to a mere 100 yards from
the hamlet. The mother ´village,` with its fine fourteenth-century
church with a fifteenth-century tower and clerestory, its large
village green and some thatched cottages, must once also have
been picturesque, but, since the 1960s, it has been swamped with
modern housing and commercial development, which have made
its character suburban. The name Houghton Regis is of Saxon
origin, its first part meaning ´settlement on a hill` and its second
denoting that it was a royal manor and it was this which saved
the village from being sacked when visited by William the
Conqueror soon after the Battle of Hastings. This was also the
reason for nearby Dunstable (which then belonged to the manor)
being chosen as the site for Henry I´s palace and priory, of which
Dunstable´s present magnificent church was only a small part. In
more recent times, the chalk, on which the village is built,
brought it renewed prosperity, as the straw-plait made from the
white straw which grew on it, was valuable to Luton´s straw-hat
industry, while the chalk itself was quarried for making cement.**

Turn right onto the A5120, passing the ´Old Red Lion`, then, after
250 yards, turn left by a signpost onto path HR45. (NB When
surveyed, the entrance to this path was obstructed, but it is hoped
that the obstruction will have been removed before publication. If it
is, however, still obstructed, climb over the padlocked gates a few
yards to your left). Now bear half left over a rise to reach the
corner of a fence, then bear half left again and follow it to a field
corner. Here go straight on, following a left-hand hedge at first.
Where the hedge turns left, bear slightly right across the field to
pass through a gap in the corner of a hedge and follow the left-

117

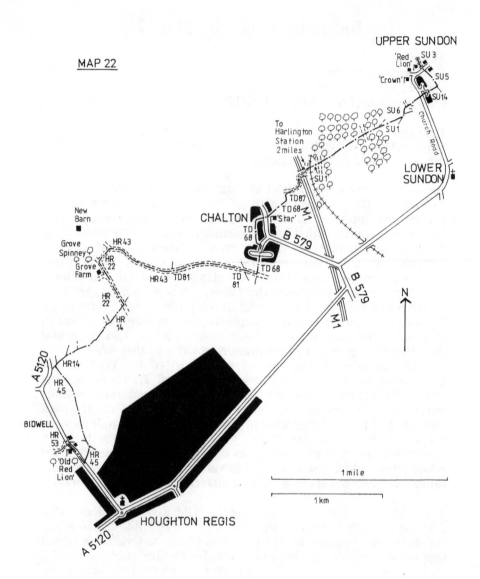

MAP 22

UPPER SUNDON

'Red Lion'   SU 3
'Crown'   SU5
SU14

SU6
To Harlington Station 2 miles   SU1
Church Road
SU1
LOWER SUNDON

TD87
TD68
CHALTON   TD68   'Star'
New Barn   TD 68   M1
B 579
Grove Spinney   HR43
Grove Farm   HR 22   B 579
HR43   TD81   TD 81   TD68   M1
HR 22

N

HR 14

A 5120   HR14
HR 45
BIDWELL
HR 53
HR 45
'Old Red Lion'

1 mile

1 km

HOUGHTON REGIS

A 5120

hand field boundary to the far end of the field. Here cross a foot-bridge and stile and turn right onto path HR14, following the right-hand hedge and stream, soon crossing another footbridge. Now continue to follow the right-hand stream and an increasingly sporadic hedge through four more fields, until you reach a cross-ing powerline. Here turn left onto bridleway HR22, following a grassy track between a left-hand hedge and the powerline to Grove Farm, then continuing straight on. On nearing a corner of Grove Spinney, fork right, following a hedge uphill, entering a green lane.

At the top of the low ridge, where views open out towards the Sundon Hills ahead and Toddington to your left, turn right onto byway HR43, following a green lane uphill, then continuing along the ridge (later on byway TD81) for three-quarters of a mile with superb views to right and left for much of the way. 120 yards after a crossing powerline, turn left over a footbridge and through a hedge gap onto path TD68, then bear slightly left across a field to enter an alleyway just right of the tallest house on the edge of Chalton and emerge at a road junction. Now go straight on downhill, then, at a right-hand bend, opposite a bungalow called ´Drumlin`, turn left onto the continuation of path TD68, following an enclosed path to a macadam drive. Turn right onto this, then, by stables, where a thatched cottage comes into view ahead, fork left along an enclosed path, passing the thatched cottage and through a kissing-gate. Now cross a drive to reach a children´s playground, then bear right, following its right-hand edge to enter a macadamed alleyway which leads you out to the B579 opposite the ´Star`.

Chalton - Upper Sundon (Map 22)

Maps
OS Landranger Sheet 166
OS Explorer Sheet 193
OS Pathfinder Sheet 1072 (TL02/12)

Parking
On-street parking is possible in residential roads off the B579 in Chalton. Do not use the pub car park without the landlord´s permission.

Chalton is today best known for its large electricity sub-station, which together with the sewage works and nearby quarries and landfill sites, disfigures what must once have been a highly

attractive area. Traditionally a remote hamlet of Toddington on the Luton road with some attractive cottages, Chalton, which has grown due to postwar housing developments, has recently gained its independence.

Cross the B579 and bear slightly left, passing the left-hand corner of the 'Star' to reach a kissing-gate in the back left-hand corner of its car park. Now take path TD68 straight on, keeping right of a line of trees and following them through scrub to cross a footbridge. Now turn left onto path TD87, following the stream to a field corner, then turning right and following a left-hand hedge to a farm road. Take this road straight on, soon bearing left then right to cross a bridge over the M1, then bearing left again. Under a powerline, turn right through a fence gap and down a flight of steps to cross a stile, then climb more steps to reach a railway crossing on the St. Pancras main line.

Cross this railway very carefully, listening for the quivering of the rails which signals the approach of a train which may not yet be in sight. Now cross a stile and take path SU1, bearing slightly left across a field to pass through a gap in a line of poplar trees by a marker post. Here cross a concrete road and bear slightly left across a field, passing right of a pylon to reach the far left-hand corner of the field. Now go straight on into scrubland, where you cross a chalky track and continue beneath a powerline. At a fork ignore a branching path to your right and continue uphill through scrub, disregarding a branching path to your left. Just before leaving the scrub, keep right at a fork to leave it by an electricity pole, then follow a left-hand fence straight on for 200 yards, until you reach a marker post, where there are views to your right across Luton towards Blows Down. Here turn left through a hedge gap and take path SU6, descending a steep bank to the floor of an old chalkpit, soon climbing a flight of steps to a hedge gap leading to a road. Cross this road and go through a fence gap opposite, then bear slightly right across a field to a hedge gap right of a gap in the houses at Upper Sundon leading to Church Road.

Now go straight on through an alleyway into a small estate, then continue to the end of the cul-de-sac. Here cross a concealed stile and take path SU14 (the line of which is under review, so please heed the waymarks!), currently following a right-hand fence along the edge of a recreation ground to reach a kissing-gate in it. Here turn left onto path SU5, heading for the right-hand end of the 'Red Lion' to reach a kissing-gate. Now continue past a pond, then bear slightly left across the green to cross Harlington Road right of the 'Red Lion'.

Upper Sundon - Sundon Hills Country Park (Map 23)

Maps
OS Landranger Sheet 166
OS Explorer Sheet 193
OS Pathfinder Sheet 1072 (TL02/12)

Parking
There is a car park at Sundon Hills Country Park and limited on-street parking is also possible in Upper Sundon.

Upper Sundon on a plateau half a mile north of Lower Sundon in its hollow above the source of the River Lea, is the much larger of the two hamlets. As Lower Sundon is, however, the location of the parish church and manor house, this suggests that it was the site of the original settlement, but that it became a ´closed village` to escape the cost of the Poor Law and its displaced population settled instead in Upper Sundon, which was probably an upland common. Sundon´s large thirteenth-century church is notable for its mediæval murals and stone seats around its walls for the elderly and infirm from before the introduction of pews (from which the phrase ´the weak go to the wall` derives). In 1653 this church briefly gained historical significance, as it was the setting of the wedding of William Foster, a persecutor of the non-conformist author and preacher, John Bunyan, and Anne Wingate, sister of the magistrate, who later imprisoned Bunyan in Bedford Gaol.

Take bridleway SU3 straight on past the right-hand side of the ´Red Lion` and along a rough lane to gates into a field, then take a stone track straight on downhill to the entrance to a sewage works. Here fork right through gates into a field and bear slightly left across it to a bridlegate left of its far corner. Do **not** go through this, but, rejoining the Icknield Way long-distance path, turn right onto path SU20 through a hedge gap in the field corner, where fine views open out ahead towards Harlington and Ampthill beyond. Here turn right and follow the hedge uphill to a field corner, then turn left beside the top hedge with superb views across Bedfordshire to your left, now including Toddington over your left shoulder. At the far side of the field, go straight on through a kissing-gate onto Harlington Road, where you turn right, then, after 200 yards, turn left into the Sundon Hills Country Park car park.

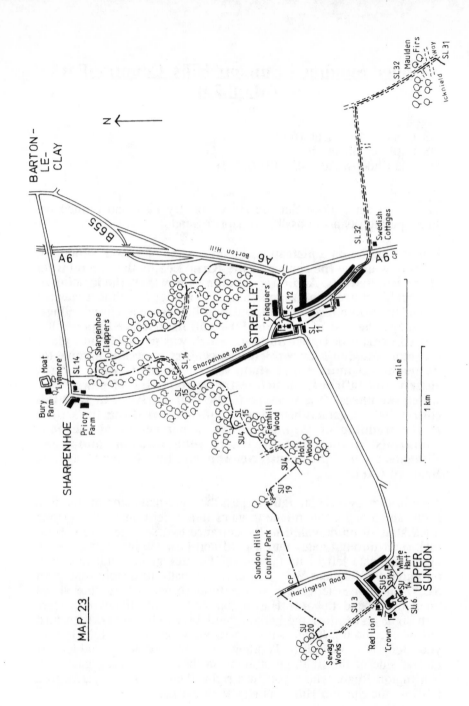

MAP 23

Sundon Hills Country Park - Sharpenhoe Clappers (Map 23)

Maps
OS Landranger Sheet 166
OS Explorer Sheet 193
OS Pathfinder Sheets 1048 (TL03/13) & 1072 (TL02/12)

Parking
There are car parks at Sundon Hills Country Park and on Sharpenhoe Road near Sharpenhoe Clappers.

Sundon Hills Country Park with its chalk downland rich in flora and superb views towards Sharpenhoe Clappers and across the Bedfordshire lowlands to the north is today a justifiably popular destination for visitors from nearby towns, to which public access was gained only thanks to its purchase by Bedfordshire County Council. In the seventeenth century the surrounding countryside was, however, the scene of critical events in the life of John Bunyan, who was arrested at Lower Samshill in 1660. Bunyan subsequently appeared before the magistrate, Francis Wingate at his sixteenth-century manor house in Harlington before being incarcerated for twelve years in Bedford Gaol where he wrote his 'Pilgrim's Progress', for which he is still famous today. Indeed, it is thought that these hills and the Barton Hills to the east were the inspiration for his reference there to 'the Delectable Mountains' and this is why they form part of the John Bunyan Trail, with which this section of the Chiltern Way coincides.

Now bear slightly left across the car park and take a permissive path by a red bin leading to a kissing-gate, then, with fine views ahead towards Sharpenhoe Clappers and to your left across the Bedfordshire lowlands, bear right to join a grassy track, following the top hedge of this large downland field. At the far end of the field, go through a kissing-gate, then bear right onto a grassy track, following a right-hand fence round the rim of a steep-sided coombe, then uphill and bearing right to reach a gate. Here fork right over a stile onto path SU19, following a left-hand hedge gently uphill with fine views behind you. At the far side of the field, turn left through a hedge gap onto path SU4, following the outside edge of Holt Wood straight on, then, at the far end of the wood, bear half left onto a farm track leading to a corner of Fernhill Wood. Here bear half left again with fine views ahead towards Harlington. At the next corner of this wood, turn right, leaving the track, and follow the outside edge of the wood to the far side of the field. Here ignore a path into the wood and turn left, still following the outside edge of the wood. After 120 yards, by a marker post, you finally enter the wood and bear left to reach a waymarked junction at the top of some steps. Here turn right onto path SL15 and follow it straight on for 350 yards, ignoring branching paths to left and right and soon skirting the top edge of a deep coombe. At a waymarked fork where gates can be seen to your right, keep straight on, following the rim of the coombe, gradually bearing left and eventually crossing a stile, where there is a fine view ahead towards Harlington. Now bear slightly right, soon crossing a second stile, where fine views open out to your left towards Harlington, Sharpenhoe and Pulloxhill in the foreground and Ampthill beyond. Now go straight across the field to a stile and steps down to Sharpenhoe Road.

Cross this and take path SL14 straight on through a car park and a gap by a gate, then along a macadamed track. On passing through a gap by another gate, take a stone track along the edge of the scrub, gradually bearing left. By a marker post, leaving the Icknield Way long-distance path, keep left, entering the scrub, then, on emerging from the scrub, where a superb view opens out to your left towards Toddington, Harlington and Sharpenhoe, go straight on to reach the near left-hand corner of the mature beech copse within the ancient earthworks on Sharpenhoe Clappers known as Clappers Wood.

Sharpenhoe Clappers - Streatley (Map 23)

Maps
OS Landranger Sheet 166
OS Explorer Sheet 193
OS Pathfinder Sheets 1048 (TL03/13) & 1072 (TL02/12)

Parking
There is a car park on Sharpenhoe Road near Sharpenhoe Clappers

The name Sharpenhoe Clappers is of mixed origin, as the village name of Sharpenhoe is Saxon, meaning ´sharp spur of land`, while Clappers comes from Norman French meaning ´rabbit warren`. While the village at the foot of the hill, which unusually has always been a hamlet of the hilltop village of Streatley, may

therefore have originated in Saxon times, the hill shows much earlier signs of habitation, as it is capped by an Iron Age hill fort and both Iron Age and Roman pottery have been found there, but the Normans adapted it for breeding rabbits and thus arose the second part of its name. Clappers Wood within the earthworks, though ancient in appearance, was, in fact, only planted between 1834 and 1844 and a painting from 1815 shows it completely bare. In the wood is an obelisk erected by W.A. Robertson in memory of his two brothers who were killed in the First World War and this was also his reason for donating the Clappers to the National Trust in 1939. The former moated manor near Bury Farm just north of the village below was home to both the leading seventeenth-century mathematician, Edmund Wingate and Thomas Norton (1532 - 1584), the Calvinist zealot, who was both Solicitor General to Elizabeth I, nicknamed 'Rackmaster General' due to his ready use of torture against Roman Catholics, and a poet and playwright credited with being the forerunner of and model for Shakespeare and Marlowe.

Now continue between a fence and the earthwork to the far end of Clappers Wood. Here fork right onto a permissive path, immediately bearing right to join a parallel path within the copse, which you follow round the inside edge of two further sides of the mature beechwood, then fork left down a steep bank and take a path straight on through scrubland. On reaching a bridlegate and kissing-gate to your left, turn left through the kissing-gate and follow a worn winding path across open downland with superb views to your left across Barton-le-Clay and the Barton Hills. Having rejoined the Icknield Way long-distance path, another kissing-gate eventually leads you into a field, where you turn left and follow a left-hand fence, then the edge of scrubland to a field corner. Here bear left, passing through a hedge gap, then take a fenced grassy track straight on. On reaching gates in the left-hand fence, turn left through a kissing-gate and descend steeply through scrubland, soon bearing right and following the contours of the hill. Eventually you descend two flights of steps to a kissing-gate, then bear slightly left across a field to a kissing-gate and footbridge at the foot of the A6 Barton Hill embankment. Here bear half right up the embankment to a fence gap by a signpost leading to the fenced roadside footway.

Turn right onto this and follow it uphill for a third of a mile to a roundabout on the edge of Streatley. Just before the roundabout, turn right onto a macadam path which joins Church Road leading into the village to reach a T-junction near the 'Chequers'.

125

Streatley - Icknield Way (Maulden Firs)
(Map 23)

Maps
OS Landranger Sheet 166
OS Explorer Sheet 193
OS Pathfinder Sheet 1072 (TL02/12)

Parking
Limited on-street parking is possible in Streatley village and there is a northbound layby on the A6 south of Swedish Cottages.

Streatley (pronounced ´Strettley` unlike its more famous Berkshire namesake and meaning ´clearing by the road)´, once comprised just a few cottages and only in the last century did it start to grow into the medium-sized village we find today. It was for this reason that, in the early twentieth century, its fourteenth-century church with its earlier font, fifteenth-century tower and a mediæval wall painting of St. Catherine, was in ruins. It was only in 1938 that the church was restored by Sir Albert Richardson and it is here that Thomas Norton was buried in 1584.

At the T-junction turn left into Sharpenhoe Road, then immediately right up a drive, passing left of the ´Chequers` to go through gates into the churchyard. Now take path SL12, forking left to pass left of the church and reach a wrought-iron gate into an alleyway. Fork left into this, taking path SL11, soon crossing the end of Churchill Close and crossing a stile into a field. Now follow the left-hand hedge straight on, descending into a dip, where you cross a stile by a gate and turn left through two more gates into Bury Lane, which leads you out to Sharpenhoe Road. Turn right onto this and follow it out of Streatley with views opening out ahead towards Galley Hill, Warden Hill and Luton, eventually reaching the A6.

Cross this road carefully and take bridleway SL32 straight on along a farm track for three-quarters of a mile with views to your right towards Galley Hill, Warden Hill and Luton, passing Swedish Cottages and later ignoring a branching track to your right. At a junction of tracks by a large metal pylon, turn right (still on bridleway SL32), following a grassy track beside a left-hand hedge towards Galley Hill. At the edge of a wood called Maulden Firs, ignore a branching track to your right and go straight on through the wood to reach the ancient Icknield Way at the point where the parallel routes of the Icknield Way long-distance path reunite.

Icknield Way (Maulden Firs) - Lilley (Map 24)

Maps
OS Landranger Sheet 166
OS Explorer Sheet 193
OS Pathfinder Sheet 1072 (TL02/12)

Parking
Limited parking is possible in Butterfield Green Road leading to Whitehill Farm.

The Icknield Way, possibly the most ancient road in Britain, which generally follows the foot of the escarpment of the Wessex Downs and Chilterns from Wiltshire to East Anglia, unusually between Dunstable and Hitchin crosses the hills to avoid the detour to pass north of the Sundon and Barton Hills. The Way, which is believed either to have been named after Boadicea´s people, the Iceni, or to be a corruption of ´ychen`, a Celtic word for cattle which may have been driven along it, is thought originally to have consisted of a number of parallel routes, of which the one or, in some places, two routes shown on modern maps are merely the survivors. The modern Icknield Way long-distance path with its various alternative routes, three of which meet at this point, is therefore very much in the tradition of its ancient namesake.

Galley Hill, which you are about to climb, has an equally long history as one of the ancient barrows scattered across it was found to contain both fourth-century and neolithic corpses. Its name, however, is a corruption of ´Gallows Hill`, as, in addition to these ancient burials, the barrow also contained the remains of fifteenth-century gallows victims.

At the crossways, take bridleway SL31 straight on, following a grassy track at first. After 60 yards, at the far side of the second hedge gap to your right, bear half right off the track and follow the edge of a left-hand belt of scrub, then keep straight on across a golf course fairway (beware of golfers driving from your left!) to a bridlegate into scrubby downland. Here take the worn path straight on up Galley Hill. At the top, where superb panoramic views open out over Luton and Streatley to your right and the hills on the North Hertfordshire border to your left, keep straight on, soon passing through a bridlegate and following a right-hand fence towards Warden Hill ahead. At a field corner, where a gate and stile

127

lead back onto the downland, do not use these, but turn left and continue to follow the right-hand fence until you reach crossing bridleway SL27. Turn right onto this, entering a sunken way. After 120 yards, where a left-hand fence begins, turn left through a kissing-gate and take a permissive path, bearing half left up Warden Hill. At the top of the ridge by a marker post, joining path SL28, bear slightly left, keeping left at a fork and climbing to a kissing-gate at a junction of fences. Now follow a left-hand fence straight on along the top of the ridge with superb views to your right across Luton. Near the far end of the ridge, where the fence turns left, leave it and go straight on across open downland, aiming towards a church with a short pointed steeple on the skyline at Stopsley, passing left of some earthworks, then continuing downhill to reach a path leading down through hillside scrub to crossing path SL26 near the bottom.

Turn left onto this and on emerging from the scrub, turn right through a kissing-gate and follow the left-hand side of a winding sporadic hedge with more views to your right across Luton. On reaching a farm road, turn right onto it, rejoining bridleway SL31, and follow it beside a right-hand hedge with fine views to your left towards Telegraph Hill, until you reach a crossing farm road. Here go straight on between large concrete blocks and follow a farm road straight on for half a mile, passing Whitehill Wood to your left and reaching the end of Butterfield Green Road by the entrance to Whitehill Farm.

Take this road straight on. After 50 yards by a telephone pole, turn left over a concealed stile onto path LU26, bearing half left across a field and soon becoming path SL34. In the far corner of the field, cross a stile and bear slightly left across the next field, passing just right of an oak tree to reach a gap in the bottom hedge with fine views ahead in mid-field across Lilley Bottom and Lilley towards Great Offley on the next ridge. Go straight on through a gap in the bottom hedge and, now in North Hertfordshire, take path LL3, following a left-hand hedge, then the edge of Lilley Park Wood straight on. At the far end of the wood, now on path LL2, continue along a green lane, eventually emerging into the car park of Lilley Village Hall. Go straight on through this car park to reach the village street, then turn left onto its footway.

Lilley - Hollybush Hill (Map 24)

Maps
OS Landranger Sheet 166
OS Explorer Sheet 193
OS Pathfinder Sheet 1072 (TL02/12)

Parking
There is a large car park by Lilley Village Hall and limited on-street parking is possible in the cul-de-sac village streets leading to the 'Silver Lion` and 'Lilley Arms`.

Lilley, situated just off the A505 (Luton - Hitchin main road), is clearly recognisable as an old estate village with a large number of its cottages bearing the rampant silver lion crest of the Docwra (pronounced 'Dockray`) and later the Sowerby families, both of Cumbrian origin, who, at various times, owned nearby Putteridge Bury. The former twelfth-century church was almost entirely rebuilt by Thomas Jekyll in 1870, but retains the Norman chancel arch and fifteenth-century font of the original building. In the seventeenth century, Lilley was a centre of non-conformity, being home to the religious writer, James Janeway, and it is believed that John Bunyan, author of 'Pilgrim's Progress`, secretly preached in the cellar of one of the village cottages. An infamous later resident of the village was the nineteenth-century alchemist, Johann Kellerman, who disappeared from Lilley as suddenly as he came.

After 60 yards, opposite the near corner of Lilley churchyard, turn right onto enclosed path LL4, soon reaching a kissing-gate into a field. Here go straight on, following a left-hand fence at first, then continuing across the field to cross a stile left of an oak tree. Now bear half right across the next field to cross a stile in the far corner. Here bear left, keeping right of a hedge and following it over the Lilley Hoo ridge, at the top of which was once open downland with an eighteenth-century racecourse where the Prince Regent (later King George IV) raced his horses. At the top of the ridge, fine views open out towards Great Offley ahead and down Lilley Bottom to your right. Now follow the hedge downhill to reach Lilley Hoo Lane near Lilley Hoo Farm. Turn right onto this cul-de-sac road and follow it for a quarter mile, passing through a tunnel under the A505 to reach a T-junction with the old main road at the foot of Hollybush Hill, where you turn left.

Hollybush Hill - Mangrove Green (Map 24)

Maps
OS Landranger Sheet 166
OS Explorer Sheet 193
OS Pathfinder Sheet 1072 (TL02/12)

Parking
Parking is possible in Lilley Hoo Lane.

Great Offley, three-quarters of a mile to your left at the top of the Chiltern escarpment, was once an important stopping point for travellers weary from the steep climb and is still today characterised by its old coaching inns. Its location also makes it an ideal centre for walking as not only does Great Offley give access to the escarpment with its steep slopes and spectacular views, but, in addition, it offers walks in the quiet and beautiful Chiltern uplands around Lilley Bottom and Kings Walden. It is therefore hardly surprising that two leading twentieth-century walkers, Don Gresswell MBE, for more than 50 years active in walking and path protection groups and founder of the Chiltern Society's Rights of Way Group, and Ron Pigram, well-known author of London Transport walks books, chose to live here. The village also has a long history being named after King Offa II of Mercia, who is believed to have had a palace here and died here in 796. In the eighteenth century it was home to Sir Thomas Salusbury, Judge of the High Court of Admiralty, who rebuilt his home of Offley Place and the chancel of the thirteenth-century parish church with its beautiful fourteenth-century font and eighteenth-century monuments by Sir Robert Taylor and Nollekens.

After 100 yards turn right into Glebe Farm, immediately forking right onto byway OF51, a green lane right of the buildings, and continuing for over half a mile to a road called Luton White Hill. Turn right onto this, then, at a crossways in Lilley Bottom, take byway OF20 straight on for a third of a mile. Just before the garage of East Lodge, fork left through a gap onto path OF8, following the park wall of Putteridge Bury uphill for two-thirds of a mile. At the far end of the second field, by the corner of a hedge, leave the wall and bear slightly left onto path OF50, following a left-hand hedge to a gate. Go through this, pass Mangrove Hall to your left and take its macadam drive straight on to reach the end of a public road by the ´King William IV` at Mangrove Green.

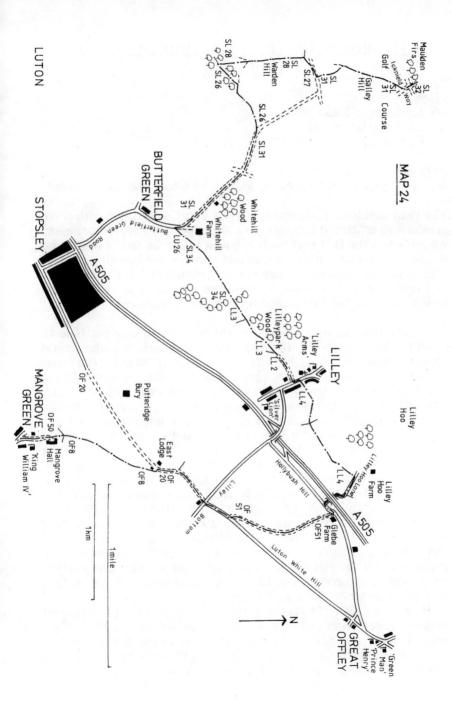

MAP 24

LUTON

Mauden
Firs
SL 32

Icknield Way

SL 31

SL 31

Golf
Course

Galley
Hill

SL 28

SL 28

Warden
Hill

SL 26

SL 27

SL 31

SL 26

SL 31

BUTTERFIELD
GREEN

Butterfield Green Road

SL 31

Whitehill
Wood

Whitehill
Farm

LU 26

SL 34

SL 26
34

LL3

Lilleypark
Wood

LL3

LL2

'Lilley
Arms'

LILLEY

LL4

'Silver
Lion'

Lilley
Hoo

STOPSLEY

A 505

OF 20

Putteridge
Bury

MANGROVE
GREEN

OF 50

Mangrove
Hall

OF 8

'King
William IV'

OF 8

East
Lodge

OF
20

OF
20

Lilley Bottom

Hollybush Hill

Lilley Hoo

Lilley
Hoo
Farm

LL4

Glebe
Farm
OF 51

OF
51

A 505

Luton White Hill

1km

1mile

N

GREAT
OFFLEY

'Green
Man'

'Prince
Henry'

131

Mangrove Green - Breachwood Green
(Map 25)

Maps
OS Landranger Sheet 166
OS Explorer Sheet 193
OS Pathfinder Sheet 1072 (TL02/12)

Parking
On-street parking is possible at Mangrove Green and Cockernhoe.

The twin hamlets of Mangrove Green and Cockernhoe with their greens and scattered cottages give a deceptively rural impression, which belies the fact that both are now less than half a mile from the edge of Luton with its voracious appetite for building land. It is largely the existence of the county boundary which they have to thank for so far being spared the fate of nearby Stopsley, which has long been swamped by urban development.

Take this road straight on across the green and down a lane to reach Cockernhoe Green. Here, at a three-way fork, take the central option straight on, then, by a bus stop, join the priority road and follow it straight on towards Luton. Just past the last house in the village, where the edge of Luton can be seen a field's length ahead, turn left over a stile by a gate onto path OF2, ignoring a grassy track to your right and taking a path between a hedge and a fence straight on through scrub. On emerging at the edge of Brickkiln Wood, turn right into a field and then left, following the edge of the wood with views to your right towards Luton and Luton Airport, soon forking left onto a fenced path through the wood. By the corner of a left-hand field, bear right, soon emerging into the corner of a right-hand field. Here turn left, then, after 15 yards, bear left again onto a fenced path into a tree belt, soon bearing right and later bearing right again to enter a field. Now turn left and follow a left-hand hedge with more views of Luton and its airport. At the far end of the field, take a short green lane straight on, passing some cottages and following their drive straight on to a road junction by Wandon End Farm.
　　Here bear half right across a traffic island and the priority road to pass the left-hand end of a wooden fence and enter a field. Now turn left onto path KW41, following the edge of the field parallel to the road for over a third of a mile, passing Wandon End and a road junction to rejoin the road at a second junction. Here take the

Darley Hall, Breachwood Green and King's Walden road straight on. At a left-hand bend, leave the road and take bridleway KW52, following a winding grassy track straight on for 300 yards to reach the corner of a hedge. Now go through a hedge gap and follow a sporadic left-hand hedge uphill. At the next hedgeline, leave the bridleway and take path KW6, bearing slightly right across a field towards a severely lightning-damaged oak tree left of and beyond a pair of oak trees, joining the top of a grass bank left of the pair of oak trees. Now follow this bank past the lightning-damaged oak tree and a second, then, just past this, bear slightly right, descending the bank and crossing a field corner to the corner of a fence. Here follow this fence straight on at first, then, where it turns left, continue along a grass path past a large oak tree. Some 30 yards beyond this tree, bear half left across the field to a kissing-gate onto Chapel Road on the edge of Breachwood Green.

Breachwood Green - Peter's Green (Map 25)

Maps
OS Landranger Sheet 166
OS Explorer Sheets 182 & 193
OS Pathfinder Sheets 1072 (TL02/12) & 1095 (TL01/11)

Parking
On-street parking is possible at Breachwood Green.

Breachwood Green, a hamlet of King's Walden parish on a ridgetop above Lilley Bottom, would seem a very remote location when approached through the maze of lanes between Luton and Stevenage and indeed the history and appearance of the surrounding countryside would tend to confirm this, but it will not be long before you realise that the village is beneath the flightpath of the approach to Luton Airport. Despite this, however, Breachwood Green, whose name derives from the Ancient British chief Breah and whose Edwardian baptist church can boast a pulpit used by the non-conformist preacher and author, John Bunyan at nearby Bendish in 1658, makes a good centre for exploring the rolling hills around Lilley Bottom which is reminiscent of Hampden Bottom in the Chiltern heartlands but far less well-known.

Turn right onto Chapel Road, then, at a road junction, go straight on down Lye Hill. After 250 yards, at a right-hand bend, fork left onto path KW3 up a slight slope into a field. Here bear right and follow the right-hand hedge downhill. Where the hedge bears right, leave it and go straight on downhill to a hedge gap in Whiteway Bottom. Do not go through this, but turn left onto path KW51, following the field edge, later a right-hand hedge to a corner of the field. Here turn right through a hedge gap onto path KW4, going straight uphill to the corner of a hedge, then following this right-hand hedge straight on to a gap by a corner of a wood called Sellbarn's Dell. Go through this and follow the edge of the wood straight on. Where it bears left, leave it and bear slightly right across the field, passing just left of an electricity pole to cross a stile by gates in the far hedge. Here take a grassy track straight on across the next field to cross a stile by gates into Wandon Green Farm. Now go straight on, passing right of a barn and left of the farmhouse to reach a road.

Turn left onto this road, then, at a junction, turn right onto the road to Peter's Green. Take this road straight on for a mile, ignoring a turning to your left, then looking out for views of Lawrence End Park to your right and eventually reaching Peter's Green, where you keep right at a fork to reach a T-junction.

MAP 25

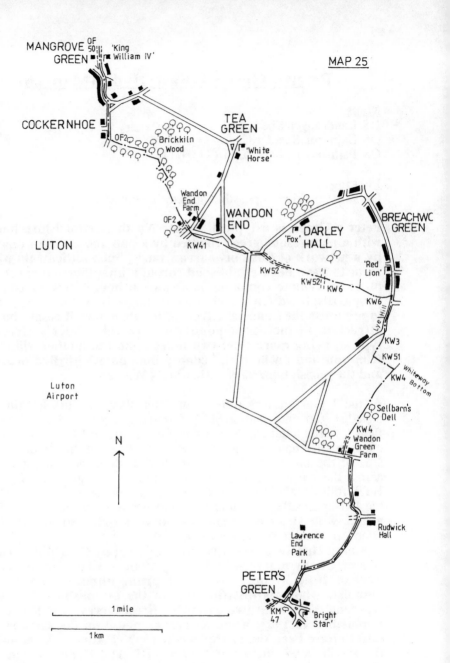

MANGROVE GREEN
OF 50
'King William IV'

COCKERNHOE

OF2

Brickkiln Wood

TEA GREEN

'White Horse'

Wandon End Farm

WANDON END

OF2

'Fox'

DARLEY HALL

BREACHWC GREEN

'Red Lion'

LUTON

KW41

KW52

KW52

KW6

KW6

Lye Hill

KW3

KW51

KW4

Whiteway Bottom

Luton Airport

N

Sellbarn's Dell

KW4
Wandon Green Farm

Rudwick Hall

Lawrence End Park

PETER'S GREEN

KM 47

'Bright Star'

1 mile

1 km

135

Peter's Green - East Hyde (Map 26)

Maps
OS Landranger Sheet 166
OS Explorer Sheet 182
OS Pathfinder Sheet 1095 (TL01/11)

Parking
On-street parking is possible at Peter's Green.

Peter's Green is a typical remote North Hertfordshire hamlet with a picturesque green flanked by a pub and cottages reached by a network of tortuous narrow lanes. Such settlements would seem to have been established through unauthorised encroach- ment on remote commons near parish boundaries by country people displaced from their home villages by landowners trying to minimise the financial effects of the Poor Law if empty houses attracted an increased population. In this, Peter's Green is typical, being more than two miles from the mother village of Kimpton and on both the county boundary with Bedfordshire and the parish boundary with King's Walden.

At the T-junction turn right, then, after 30 yards, fork left through a hedge gap onto path KM47, following a grassy track across a field towards a tall ash tree at the southern tip of Chiltern Green, an even smaller hamlet similar to Peter's Green on the Bedfordshire side of the boundary. Reentering Bedfordshire, bear slightly right across the green, then cross a gravel track and a stile and take path HY9, following a left-hand fence to cross another stile. Now follow the left-hand side of a field boundary straight on for two-thirds of a mile with views of Luton Hoo to your right and The Hyde to your left opening out at the top of a rise.

    Luton Hoo, in its extensive park laid out by Capability Brown, was originally designed in 1767 by Robert Adam for the Third Earl of Bute, George III's first prime minister and a keen botanist, who was instrumental in the establishment of Kew Gardens. Following two extensive fires, however, it had to be remodelled in 1903, while an earlier house on the same site is said to have been the birthplace in 1507 of Anne Boleyn, one of the six ill-fated queens of Henry VIII. The Hyde, though less pretentious in scale, is also of Georgian origin.

    On reaching a large clump of trees to your left, go past its right- hand end to reach a junction of tracks, then turn left onto path

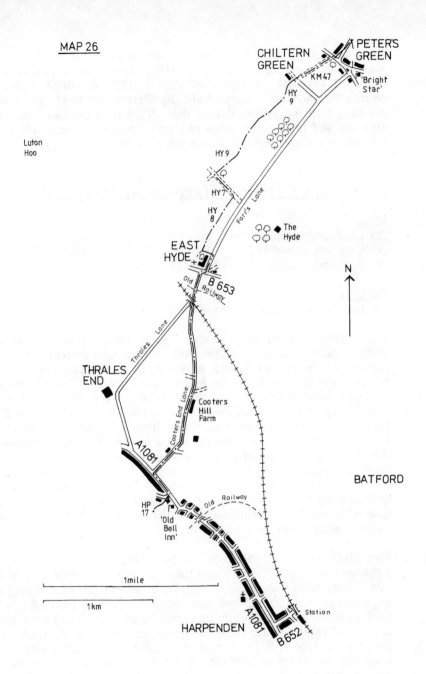

MAP 26

PETER'S GREEN

CHILTERN GREEN

KM 47

'Bright Star'

HY 9

Luton Hoo

HY 9

Farr's Lane

HY 7

HY 8

The Hyde

EAST HYDE

N

B 653

Old Railway

Thrales Lane

THRALES END

Cooters End Lane

Cooters Hill Farm

A 1081

BATFORD

Old Railway

HP 17

'Old Bell Inn'

1 mile

1 km

Station

HARPENDEN

A 1081

B 652

HY7, following a grassy track past the back of the clump. After 300 yards, turn right onto path HY8, following a grassy track downhill towards the turret of East Hyde's red-brick Italianate church in the Lea valley, built by Ferrey in 1841, eventually reaching a hedge at the edge of the village by a tall oak tree. Here turn left and follow the hedge to Farr's Lane, then turn right down it to reach a staggered crossroads with the B653.

East Hyde - Harpenden (Map 26)

Maps
OS Landranger Sheet 166
OS Explorer Sheet 182
OS Pathfinder Sheet 1095 (TL01/11)

Parking
Limited on-street parking is available at East Hyde.

The village of East Hyde, extending along the B653 in the Lea Valley, barely existed in the early nineteenth century, but the coming of the railways with no fewer than two railway stations would seem to have led to its expansion. First the Great Northern Railway built a branch line from Welwyn Garden City up the Lea Valley to Luton and Dunstable in 1860 with a station at East Hyde known as Luton Hoo and then, in 1868, the Midland Railway built their St. Pancras - Bedford main line, nicknamed the 'Bed-Pan Line', with a station at East Hyde known as Chiltern Green. While the old GNR branch line with Luton Hoo Station was closed by Dr. Beeching in 1962, the Midland Railway station had already been closed and so all that now remains is one main line with no station, but much of the old branch line has since become part of the Lea Valley Walk.

Turn right onto the B653, then left into Thrales End Lane, crossing a bridge over the River Lea and the old GNR line (now part of the Lea Valley Walk), then passing under a railway bridge carrying the St. Pancras main line. Now turn left into Cooters End Lane and, back in Hertfordshire, follow this quiet single-track road for a mile, at first climbing with views to your left towards Batford, then passing Cooters Hill Farm and descending, ignoring a turning to your left and eventually reaching the A1081 (formerly part of the A6 London-Manchester main road) on the edge of Harpenden.

Harpenden - Flamstead (Map 27)

Maps
OS Landranger Sheet 166
OS Explorer Sheet 182
OS Pathfinder Sheet 1095 (TL01/11)

Parking
On-street parking is available in Harpenden.

Harpenden, whose name is said to mean ´valley of the night-ingales,` is today a small Hertfordshire town with some 30,000 inhabitants, but local people still refer to it as ´the village`. This is, indeed, indicative of the fact that 100 years ago it still was a small village, which, till 1859, had been merely a hamlet of nearby Wheathamstead parish, but the coming of the railways - first the Great Northern Railway Dunstable branch in 1860 with a station at nearby Batford and then the Midland Railway main line in 1868 with a station near the village centre and its branch to Hemel Hempstead, known as the ´Nicky Line` - brought Harpenden within easy reach of London and so, by 1900, well-to-do commuters were starting to colonise the village. The preservation of its large common, which extends into its centre, has, however, enabled the retention of its rural atmosphere, which belies the spread of suburban villas in all directions.

Turn left onto the A1081, which is said to be of Roman origin (where Harpenden Station can be reached by continuing for 1 mile and then turning left onto the B652). After 250 yards, by a filling station, turn right into Roundwood Lane, crossing the entrance to the filling station, then forking left onto path HP17, following a raised footway past a small factory, then continuing between fences to a recreation ground. Bear half right across this to its far corner to enter a fenced path between allotments, which you follow gently uphill, crossing two roads, passing the end of a third and crossing a fourth. Now ignore the entrances to a school and its playing fields and continue until you emerge into the corner of a field. Here follow a left-hand hedge straight on, soon bearing left and later entering a short green lane. Now on path HR11, by the corner of a right-hand hedge, bear half left and follow a left-hand hedge to a gap leading to the former Midland Railway Hemel Hempstead Branch. Known as the ´Nicky Line`, it was closed to passenger traffic in 1947, but remained in use for goods trains till the 1970s and has now become a foot and cycle path from Harpenden to Hemel Hempstead.

Turn right onto the old railway, where several sleepers have been retained in its surface to show its origin, passing between safety barriers and continuing for over a quarter mile. At the end of a short macadamed section by a seat, turn right onto a crossing path, rejoining path HR11, passing through a hedge gap and following the edge of a wood to cross a stile leading onto a golf course. Now bear left and follow the edge of the wood along the edge of the golf course until a marker post directs you to enter the wood. Take the obvious path through it, eventually emerging over a stile into a field. Here turn right and pass through an outcrop of scrub, then follow a right-hand fence and sporadic hedge, ignoring a series of stiles in the fence provided for golfers to retrieve lost balls. Eventually you cross a transverse fenceline and bear left to reach a stile into a fenced lane (bridleway HR1). Take this straight on downhill past Harpenden Bury Farm, then, at a junction of tracks, turn right onto a wide gravel track, soon crossing the golf course and passing cottages and later stables to your right to reach Kinsbourne Green Lane.

Cross this road and take path HR16 straight on through a fence gap opposite, bearing slightly right across a large field to a prominent hedge gap in its far left-hand corner. Here go straight on, keeping left of a hedge and following it until it bears right, then go straight on across the field, heading for stables ahead to cross a stile in a post-and-rail fence. Now on path HR18, bear slightly left across a paddock to pass through three gates, crossing the drive to Verlam End, then turn left onto a track crossing a bridge over the River Ver.

The name Verlam End is interesting as it recalls the old name ´Verlamstead`, of which Flamstead is a corruption and although the River Ver now forms the boundary here between Harpenden Rural and Redbourn parishes, it suggests that Flamstead parish must once have extended to this point.

Now turn right onto path RB6, heading for the right-hand end of Whitehill Wood on the hillock ahead, to reach a small gate leading to the A5183 (formerly the A5, following the course of the Roman road from Dover via London, St. Albans and Dunstable to Holyhead known as Watling Street) near Junction 9 of the M1. Turn right onto its footway and at a roundabout, cross the sliproads of the M1 and take the A5 footway straight on under the motorway bridge. At a second roundabout, cross the Kinsbourne Green road, then follow the road side of the crash-barrier until you have sufficient visibility to cross the A5 dual-carriageway. Now bear left

140

MAP 27

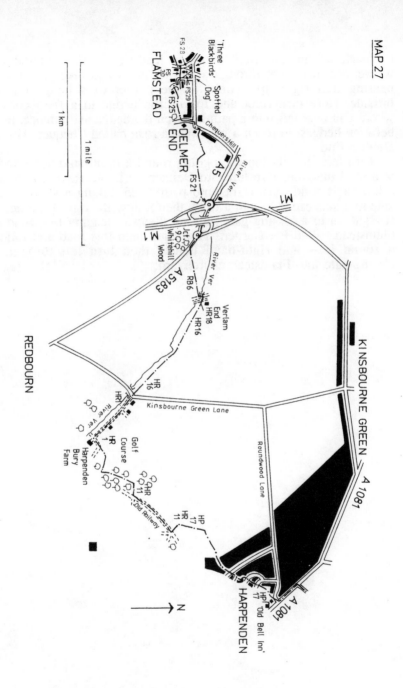

FLAMSTEAD

'Three Blackbirds'

Spotted Dog'

FS 28

FS 30

FS 29

FS 25

DELMER END

Chequers Hill

River Ver

A5

FS 21

Jct 9

M1

M1

Whitehill Wood

A5183

RB6

River Ver

Verlam End

HR18

HR16

REDBOURN

HR 16

HR

River Ver

HR 11

HR

Kinsbourne Green Lane

Golf Course

Harpenden Bury Farm

Old Railway

HR 11

HP 17

HR 11

HR

KINSBOURNE GREEN

A 1081

Roundwood Lane

HARPENDEN

HP 17

'Old Bell Inn'

A 1081

N

1 km

1 mile

141

to reach a concrete field entrance leading off the roundabout, where you turn right through a gap by gates and take path FS21, bearing half right up a field to the corner of a hedge on the hillside. Here turn right and follow the hedge to a field corner, where you bear left into a path between the hedge and a fence, later between hedges, to reach a gate onto a road called Chequers Hill at Delmer End.

Turn left onto its footway, going round a right-hand bend, then, at a road junction, turn left into Delmerend Lane. Having rounded a left-hand bend, turn right onto path FS25, taking a short green lane to a squeeze-stile into a field, then follow the right-hand hedge straight on to a kissing-gate into an alleyway leading to a road in Flamstead called Pie Garden. Turn right onto this road and follow it round left- and right-hand bends, then turn left through a kissing-gate into Flamstead churchyard.

Flamstead - Gaddesden Row (Map 28)

Maps
OS Landranger Sheet 166
OS Explorer Sheet 182
OS Pathfinder Sheet 1095 (TL01/11)
(part only) Chiltern Society FP Map No.20

Parking
Limited on-street parking is available in Flamstead.

Flamstead, a corruption of 'Verlamstead', on its hilltop above the Ver valley, has an attractive village centre with half-timbered and flint cottages and a row of almshouses dating from 1669, but is dominated, when seen from afar, by its magnificent twelfth-century church with a massive tower incorporating Roman bricks and a small mediæval spire known as a 'Hertfordshire spike'. The church also boasts some of the finest mediæval murals in Hertfordshire, which were only rediscovered in about 1930, as well as exquisite seventeenth- and eighteenth-century marble monuments by Stanton and Flaxman and is the burial place of the founder of the renowned transport firm, Thomas Pickford, who died in 1811. Despite being less than a mile from both the M1 and the A5, Flamstead has remained a remarkably quiet, rural village and, with its open, hilly surroundings, offers a selection of pleasant walks with fine views.

In the churchyard, if wishing to visit one of the village pubs or look at the attractive village centre, fork right onto path FS29 passing right of the church. Otherwise, take path FS30, the left-hand of the three paths through the churchyard, straight on to a gate and gap leading to Trowley Hill Road. Turn left onto this road, then immediately right onto path FS32, a fenced alleyway leading you out past a housing estate into a field. Now go straight on across the field, passing an electricity pole and then heading for a hedge gap left of an ash tree in tall bushes ahead. Go through this gap and turn left onto a narrow road called Pietley Hill. At a left-hand bend turn right over a stile onto path FS37, bearing slightly right downhill to cross a stile at the bottom, then continue uphill to reach the top hedge, where you turn right and follow the near side of the hedge to a gap in a field corner leading to Wood End Lane where there is a fine view behind you back across the valley to Flamstead.
  Go through this gap, then turn right into Wood End Lane. Just

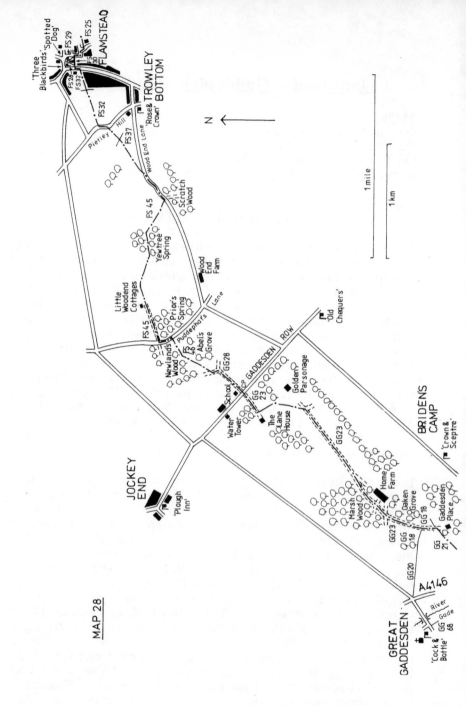

MAP 28

FLAMSTEAD

'Three Blackbirds' 'Spotted Dog'

FS28
FS29
FS25
FS30
FS32

Pietley Hill
FS37
FS32

Wood End Lane

Rose & Crown' TROWLEY BOTTOM

FS45

Scratch Wood

Yewtree Spring

Wood End Farm

Little Woodend Cottages

Prior's Spring

FS45

Newlands Wood

Puddephat's

46

Abels Grove

GG28

School

Water Tower

GG 23

The Lane House

Golden Parsonage

ROW

GP GADDESDEN

GG23

Home Farm

Marsh Wood

GG 18

Oaken Grove

Gaddesden Place

GG 21

GG 18

GG23

GG20

A4146

'Old Chequers'

BRIDENS CAMP

'Crown & Sceptre'

JOCKEY END

'Plough Inn'

GREAT GADDESDEN

River Gade

GG 68

'Cock & Bottle'

N ←

1 mile

1 km

144

after Scratch Wood begins to your left, turn right over a stile by a gate and take path FS45, bearing slightly left across a field to the near corner of a wood called Yewtree Spring. Here keep right of the wood and follow its outside edge to a stile into it. Turn left over this and follow the waymarked path through the wood, which is carpeted with bluebells in April and May, to reach a stile at the far corner into a field. Here bear slightly right across the field, with views ahead across these remote hills towards the distant Bedfordshire village of Studham, to a stile in a hedge just right of a corner of the field. Cross this and turn left, following a left-hand hedge and fence. On nearing Little Woodend Cottages, where the left-hand fence diverges from the hedge, cross a stile in the fence and keep left of a shed to join a drive by the cottages. Take this drive straight on to reach Puddephat´s Lane, then turn left onto this road and follow it through Newland´s Wood. Just after a slight left-hand bend, turn right over a stile by a gate onto path FS46, following a left-hand fence into a field, then bearing slightly left across the field, passing the corner of a copse called Abel´s Grove to reach a hedge gap in the far corner of the field. Go through this and turn left into a green lane. Where the lane forks, bear right, taking path GG28 along its continuation, eventually passing a school to your right to reach a road at Gaddesden Row.

Gaddesden Row - Gaddesden Place (Map 28)

Maps
OS Landranger Sheet 166
OS Explorer Sheet 182
OS Pathfinder Sheet 1095 (TL01/11)
Chiltern Society FP Map No.20

Parking
There is a small car park at the end of path GG28 opposite Gaddesden Row School.

Gaddesden Row is an unusual settlement, largely comprising a series of isolated farms and cottages ranged along a two-mile-long ridgetop road with the hamlet of Jockey End around the ´Plough Inn´ at its northwest end. Despite its scattered nature, Gaddesden Row would, however, seem to have been populated since the Stone Age, as Stone Age flints, tools and weapons have been found here.

By the school, cross the road and take path GG23 straight on along the drive to The Lane House. On reaching a gate and kissing-gate, turn left and follow a right-hand hedge to a field corner, where you turn right through a hedge gap and cross three stiles to enter a parkland field with a view ahead of the Golden Parsonage, the original home of the Halseys, who have held land in Great Gaddesden since 1512, of which only a wing built in 1705 remains. Now bear half right across two fields, later with fine views of the Golden Parsonage to your left, to reach a gap in the far hedge at a junction of farm tracks. Here bear half right onto a track following a right-hand hedge at first, then continuing between a fence and a belt of trees to reach a corner of Marsh Wood.

Now fork right onto a track into the wood and follow it straight on, ignoring a branching track to your right, passing Home Farm to your left and then disregarding a crossing track, to reach a gate into a field. Here take a rough track straight on, passing left of a leaning oak tree, then continuing with views to your right across the Gade valley. Soon on path GG18, cross a stile left of some gates in a slight dip and follow a right-hand fence uphill until you reach gates in the fence. Turn right through these onto path GG21, bearing half left and passing just right of a cattle trough, aiming for a cottage with a gable at Water End in the Gade valley when this comes into view, with Gaddesden Place emerging from the trees to your left. Eventually you cross a stile in the left-hand fence near the bottom left-hand corner of the field with superb views across the picturesque hamlet of Water End with its seventeenth-century brick-and-timber cottages below you and towards Great Gaddesden with its prominent church to your right.

Gaddesden Place - Potten End (Map 29)

Maps
OS Landranger Sheet 166
OS Explorer Sheet 182
OS Pathfinder Sheets 1095 (TL01/11) & 1119 (TL00/10)
Chiltern Society FP Map No.20

Parking
Limited on-street parking is available in Great Gaddesden village.

Great Gaddesden, which, like so many ´great` villages, is smaller than its ´little` namesake, is set in an idyllic location in the Gade valley, but the picturesque cluster of church, farm, inn, school and cottages is marred by an insensitive council house development tacked onto it. In the past Great Gaddesden was very much the estate village of the Halseys who have lived here since 1512, still have a large estate here and continue to live at Gaddesden Place. This Palladian mansion was built for the Halseys between 1768 and 1773 by James Wyatt, designer of Ashridge, to replace their previous house, the Golden Parsonage, of which only a wing from 1705 remains, while the church contains the eighteenth-century Halsey Chapel with over twenty monuments to family members including examples of the work of Rysbrack and Flaxman. The twelfth-century church is also noted for the use of Roman bricks from a nearby villa in its construction and its massive fifteenth-century tower with some fearsome gargoyles.

Having crossed the stile, continue downhill on path GG21, crossing another stile and bearing slightly left to reach the near left-hand corner of a cream cottage at Water End. Now follow its fence to a stile and gate onto the A4146. Cross this with great care (beware of the blind bend to your left!), then turn right onto its footway. After 10 yards, turn left onto path GG66 down an alleyway to two stiles into a riverside meadow. Here bear half right, following a right-hand fence at first to a footbridge over the Gade, then turn left, crossing another footbridge and a stile by an electricity pole. Now bear slightly right, heading for a hawthorn bush on a rise, where you join a right-hand fence and follow it, ignoring a stile in it and eventually crossing two stiles by gates to reach Nettleden Road.

Turn right onto this, then, after 90 yards, turn left over a stile onto path GG63, going straight uphill and passing left of a dead beech tree to reach a gap in the edge of Heizdin´s Wood, where you

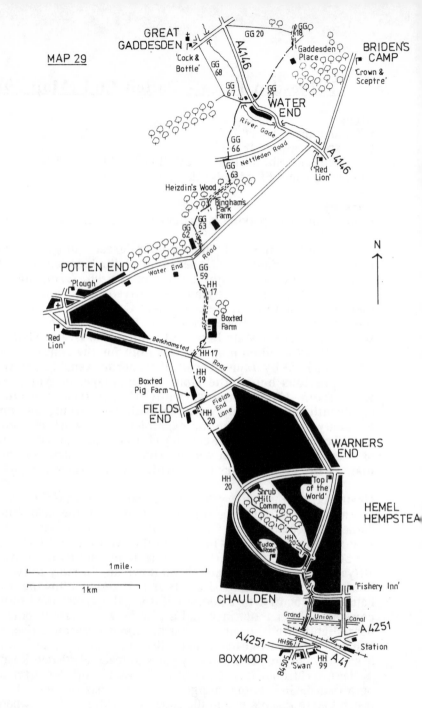

MAP 29

GREAT
GADDESDEN
'Cock &
Bottle'

GG 20
A4146

GG
68

GG
67

GG
21

GG
68

BRIDEN'S
CAMP

Gaddesden
Place

'Crown &
Sceptre'

WATER
END

A4146

River Gade

GG
66

Nettleden Road

GG
63

'Red
Lion'

Heizdin's Wood

Bingham's
Park
Farm

GG 63

GG
62

Road

POTTEN END

Water End

GG
59

'Plough'

HH
17

Boxted
Farm

'Red
Lion'

Berkhamsted

Road

HH17

HH
19

Boxted
Pig Farm

FIELDS
END

Fields
End
Lane

HH
20

WARNERS
END

HH
20

Top
of the
World'

Shrub
Hill
Common

HEMEL
HEMPSTEAD

HH
20

N

'Tudor
Rose'

1 mile

1 km

CHAULDEN

'Fishery Inn'

Grand   Union   Canal

A4251

A4251

A41

Station

BOXMOOR

HH96

HH
99

A41

B4505 'Swan'

148

should turn round for a fine view back across Water End towards Gaddesden Place. In the wood, take a wide terraced track, bearing half right, climbing gently and ignoring a crossing path. On leaving the wood, turn right through a hedge gap and head for the left-hand of two oak trees. Now bear half left, with fine views to your right across Nettleden in its peaceful valley, to reach the near end of a hedge. Here turn left onto path GG62, following the near side of the hedge to a kissing-gate in a field corner leading to a bend in a track. Bear right then left onto this track and follow it along a lane to Water End Road on the outskirts of Potten End.

Potten End - Hemel Hempstead Station (Map 29)

Maps
OS Landranger Sheet 166
OS Explorer Sheet 182
OS Pathfinder Sheet 1119 (TL00/10)
Chiltern Society FP Map No.20

Parking
Limited on-street parking is available in Potten End village, some distance from the Way and on-street parking is also possible in the suburbs of Hemel Hempstead.

Potten End, with its picturesque green surrounded by its church, a pub, the village hall and cottages, would seem the epitome of the English village, but a brief glance at a map of 1834 reveals that, in contrast to most villages which were established in Saxon times, Potten End then comprised little more than a few scattered cottages on the edge of Berkhamsted Common. Indeed, its church is Victorian and most of its houses and cottages are of even later origin and so it is really a suburban settlement which grew up when the coming of the railways and later the motor car provided easy access to London. Its name, which is shown on the 1834 map and is often the butt of jokes and the subject of speculation, probably arises from the presence of hilltop clay, which may have been used for pottery.

Turn right onto this road, then, at a right-hand bend, turn left through a bridlegate onto narrow fenced path GG59 and continue to a stile into a field. Now follow the right-hand fence straight on, passing a tall oak tree, then continuing between the fence and a left-hand hedge to a stile in the valley bottom. Here turn left onto path HH17, following a fenced cattle track, soon turning right over a stile by a gate and following the track uphill to Boxted Farm. Where the track turns left into the farm, go straight on through a small gap left of double gates and follow the left-hand fence past the farm, then bearing right and later left to reach a stile onto the farm drive. Here turn right onto the drive and follow it to Berkhamsted Road, then take path HH19, going through a kissing-gate by a gate opposite and bearing half left across a field to a corner of a fence left of Boxted Pig Farm. Now follow this fence straight on to cross a stile into an area of scrub, through which you keep straight on. Under a powerline, bear right between hedges to reach a squeeze-stile leading to Fields End Lane at Fields End.

Turn right onto this road. After 100 yards, just before a pair of cottages to your left, turn left onto path HH20, following a mac-adam drive at first, then continuing between hedges for over half a mile, ignoring all hedge gaps and branching or crossing paths, soon skirting Hemel Hempstead and eventually reaching a crossing road called Long Chaulden. Cross this, bearing slightly right and continue on path HH20, passing between safety barriers, then lined by hedges, soon entering woodland on Shrub Hill Common. After a quarter mile, at a major crossways in a clearing with a rough meadow to your left and a mown recreation ground to your right, bear half right onto the second crossing path (still HH20), following the inside edge of the wood. On eventually emerging onto the recreation ground, keep straight on, passing left of a children's playground, then bear slightly right to reach a road junction.

Here join the major road (Jocketts Road) and follow it uphill to a mini-roundabout. Now turn right and take Northridge Way downhill, going straight on at the first mini-roundabout, then turning right at the second into Chaulden Lane, immediately forking left into Old Fishery Lane. Take this quiet cul-de-sac downhill, crossing a bridge over the picturesque Grand Union Canal. At the end of the road, go straight on through gates and under the West Coast main line and A41. At the far end of the tunnel, go through gates, then turn left through a kissing-gate onto path HH96, following a left-hand fence to a kissing-gate onto the A4251. Turn left onto its footway, then, **if wishing to continue southwards on the Chiltern Way**, just before a series of bridges, cross the A4251 and take fenced path HH99 leading off the end of a short cul-de-sac opposite. Now turn back to p.15 for the continuation. **Otherwise, for Hemel Hempstead Station**, continue under the bridges to a roundabout, then turn right for the station.

INDEX OF PLACE NAMES

Place	Sections
Tom's Hill	18
Tring	18
Trowley Bottom	28
Turville	8
Turville Heath	9
Tylers Green	5
Upper Maidensgrove	9/11
Upper Sundon	22/23
Verlam End	27
Wandon End	25
Warden Hill	24
Warners End	29
Water End (Herts.)	29
Wendover Dean	16
Wendover Station	15/16
Whipsnade	20
Whipsnade Down	20
Wigginton	17/18
Wigginton Bottom	17/18
Winchmore Hill	4
Wormsley Valley	12

Books Published by
THE BOOK CASTLE

**CHANGES IN OUR LANDSCAPE: Aspects of Bedfordshire,
Buckinghamshire and the Chilterns 1947-1992**: Eric Meadows.
Over 350 photographs from the author's collection spanning nearly 50 years.
**COUNTRYSIDE CYCLING IN BEDFORDSHIRE, BUCKINGHAMSHIRE
AND HERTFORDSHIRE**: Mick Payne.
Twenty rides on and off-road for all the family.
**PUB WALKS FROM COUNTRY STATIONS: Bedfordshire and
Hertfordshire**: Clive Higgs.
Fourteen circular country rambles, each starting and finishing at a railway station
and incorporating a pub stop at a mid way point.
**PUB WALKS FROM COUNTRY STATIONS: Buckinghamshire and
Oxfordshire**: Clive Higgs.
Circular rambles incorporating pub-stops.
LOCAL WALKS: South Bedfordshire and North Chilterns: Vaughan
Basham.
Twenty-seven thematic circular walks.
LOCAL WALKS: North and Mid Bedfordshire: Vaughan Basham.
Twenty-five thematic circular walks.
FAMILY WALKS: Chilterns South: Nick Moon. Thirty 3 to 5 mile circular
walks.
FAMILY WALKS: Chilterns North: Nick Moon. Thirty shorter circular
walks.
CHILTERN WALKS:Hertfordshire,Bedfordshire and North Bucks:
Nick Moon.
CHILTERN WALKS: Buckinghamshire: Nick Moon.
CHILTERN WALKS: Oxfordshire and West Buckinghamshire:
Nick Moon.
A trilogy of circular walks, in association with the Chiltern Society. Each
volume contains 30 circular walks.
OXFORDSHIRE WALKS: Oxford, the Cotswolds and the Cherwell Valley:
OXFORDSHIRE WALKS: Oxford, the Downs and the Thames Valley:
Both by Nick Moon.
Two volumes that complement Chiltern Walks: Oxfordshire, and complete
coverage of the county, in association with the Oxford Fieldpaths Society. Thirty
circular walks in each.
THE D'ARCY DALTON WAY:
Nick Moon.
Long-distance footpath across the Oxfordshire Cotswolds and Thames Valley,
with various circular walk suggestions.

THE CHILTERN WAY: Nick Moon.
A guide to the new 133 mile circular Long-Distance-Path through Bedfordshire, Buckinghamshire, Hertfordshire and Oxfordshire, as planned by the Chiltern Society.

JOURNEYS INTO BEDFORDSHIRE: Anthony Mackay.
Foreword by The Marquess of Tavistock, Woburn Abbey. A lavish book of over 150 evocative ink drawings.

JOURNEYS INTO BUCKINGHAMSHIRE: Anthony Mackay.
Superb line drawings plus background text: large format landscape gift book.

BUCKINGHAMSHIRE MURDERS: Len Woodley.
Nearly two centuries of nasty crimes.

WINGRAVE: A Rothschild Village in the Vale: Margaret and Ken Morley.
Thoroughly researched and copiously illustrated survey of the last 200 years in this lovely village between Aylesbury and Leighton Buzzard.

HISTORIC FIGURES IN THE BUCKINGHAMSHIRE LANDSCAPE: John Houghton.
Major personalities and events that have shaped the county's past, including a special section on Bletchley Park.

TWICE UPON A TIME: John Houghton.
North Bucks short stories loosely based on fact.

SANCTITY AND SCANDAL IN BEDS AND BUCKS: John Houghton.
A miscellany of unholy people and events.

MANORS and MAYHEM, PAUPERS and PARSONS: Tales from Four Shires:Beds., Bucks., Herts. and Northants: John Houghton.
Little known historical snippets and stories.

MYTHS and WITCHES, PEOPLE and POLITICS:
Tales from Four Shires: Bucks.,Beds., Herts. and Northants:
John Houghton.
Anthology of strange, but true historical events.

FOLK: Characters and Events in the History of Bedfordshire and Northamptonshire: Vivienne Evans.
Anthology of people of yesteryear-arranged alphabetically by village or town.

JOHN BUNYAN: His Life and Times: Vivienne Evans.
Highly praised and readable account

THE RAILWAY AGE IN BEDFORDSHIRE: Fred Cockman.
Classic, illustrated account of early railway history.

A LASTING IMPRESSION: Michael Dundrow.
A boyhood evacuee recalls his years in the Chiltern village of Totternhoe near Dunstable.

GLEANINGS REVISITED: Nostalgic Thoughts of a Bedfordshire Farmer's Boy: E.W.O'Dell.
His own sketches and early photographs adorn this lively account of rural Bedfordshire in days gone by.

BEDFORDSHIRE'S YESTERYEARS Vol 2: The Rural Scene: Brenda Fraser-Newstead.
Vivid first-hand accounts of country life two or three generations ago.
BEDFORDSHIRE'S YESTERYEARS Vol 3: Craftsmen and Tradespeople: Brenda Fraser-Newstead.
Fascinating recollections over several generations practising many vanishing crafts and trades
BEDFORDSHIRE'S YESTERYEARS Vol 4: War Times and Civil Matters: Brenda Fraser-Newstead.
Two World Wars, plus transport, law and order, etc.
PROUD HERITAGE: A Brief History of Dunstable, 1000-2000AD: Vivienne Evans.
Century by century account of the town's rich tradition and key events, many of national significance.
DUNSTABLE WITH THE PRIORY: 1100-1550: Vivienne Evans.
Dramatic growth of Henry 1's important new town around a major crossroads.
DUNSTABLE IN TRANSITION: 1550-1700: Vivienne Evans.
Wealth of original material as the town evolves without the Priory.
DUNSTABLE DECADE: THE EIGHTIES: A Collection of Photographs: Pat Lovering.
A souvenir book of nearly 300 pictures of people and events in the 1980s.
STREETS AHEAD: An Illustrated Guide to the Origins of Dunstable's Street Names: Richard Walden.
Fascinating text and captions to hundreds of photographs, past and present, throughout the town.
DUNSTABLE IN DETAIL: Nigel Benson.
A hundred of the town's buildings and features, plus town trail map.
OLD DUNSTABLE: Bill Twaddle.
A new edition of this collection of early photographs.
BOURNE and BRED: A Dunstable Boyhood Between the Wars: Colin Bourne.
An elegantly written, well illustrated book capturing the spirit of the town over fifty years ago.
OLD HOUGHTON: Pat Lovering.
Pictorial record capturing the changing appearances of Houghton Regis over the past 100 years.
ROYAL HOUGHTON: Pat Lovering.
Illustrated history of Houghton Regis from the earliest of times to the present.
THE STOPSLEY BOOK: James Dyer.
Definitive, detailed account of this historic area of Luton. Includes 150 rare photographs.
THE STOPSLEY PICTURE BOOK: James Dyer.
A wealth of new material and photographs make an ideal companion to The Stopsley Book.

PUBS and PINTS: The Story of Luton's Public Houses and Breweries: Stuart Smith.
The background to beer in the town, plus hundreds of photographs, old and new.

LUTON AT WAR 1
As compiled by the Luton News in 1947, a well illustrated thematic account.

THE CHANGING FACE OF LUTON: An Illustrated History: Stephen Bunker, Robin Holgate and Marian Nichols.
Luton's development from earliest times to the present busy, industrial town. Illustrated in colour and mono.

WHERE THEY BURNT THE TOWN HALL DOWN: Luton, The First World War and the Peace Day Riots, July 1919: Dave Craddock.
Detailed analysis of a notorious incident.

THE MEN WHO WORE STRAW HELMETS: Policing Luton, 1840-1974: Tom Madigan.
Fine chronicled history, many rare photographs; author served in Luton Police for fifty years.

BETWEEN THE HILLS: The Story of Lilley, a Chiltern Village: Roy Pinnock.
A priceless piece of our heritage- the rural beauty remains but the customs and way of life described here have largely disappeared.

KENILWORTH SUNSET: A Luton Town Supporter's Journal: Tim Kingston.
Frank and funny account of football's ups and downs.

A HATTER GOES MAD!: Kristina Howells.
Luton Town footballers, officials and supporters talk to a female fan.

LEGACIES: Tales and Legends of Luton and the North Chilterns: Vic Lea.
Mysteries and stories based on fact, including Luton Town Football Club. Many photographs.

THREADS OF TIME: Shela Porter.
The life of a remarkable mother and businesswoman, spanning the entire century and based in Hitchin and (mainly) Bedford.

LEAFING THROUGH LITERATURE: Writers' Lives in Herts and Beds: David Carroll.
Illustrated short biographies of many famous authors and their connections with these counties.

A PILGRIMAGE IN HERTFORDSHIRE: H.M.Alderman.
Classic, between-the-wars tour round the county, embellished with line drawings.

THE VALE OF THE NIGHTINGALE: Molly Andrews.
Several generations of a family, lived against a Harpenden backdrop.

SUGAR MICE AND STICKLEBACKS: Childhood Memories of a Hertfordshire Lad: Harry Edwards.
Vivid evocation of gentle pre-war in an archetypal village, Hertingfordbury.

SWANS IN MY KITCHEN: Lis Dorer.
Story of a Swan Sanctuary near Hemel Hempstead.

THE HILL OF THE MARTYR: An Architectural History of St.Albans Abbey: Eileen Roberts.
Scholarly and readable chronological narrative history of Hertfordshire and Bedfordshire's famous cathedral. Fully illustrated with photographs and plans.
CHILTERN ARCHAEOLOGY: RECENT WORK:A Handbook for the Next Decade: edited by Robin Holgate.
The latest views, results and excavations by twenty-three leading archaeologists throughout the Chilterns.
THE TALL HITCHIN INSPECTOR'S CASEBOOK: A Victorian Crime Novel Based on Fact: Edgar Newman.   Worthies of the time encounter more archetypal villains.

SPECIALLY FOR CHILDREN

VILLA BELOW THE KNOLLS: A Story of Roman Britain: Michael Dundrow.
An exciting adventure for young John in Totternhoe and Dunstable two thousand years ago.
THE RAVENS: One Boy Against the Might of Rome: James Dyer.
On the Barton Hills and in the south-east of England as the men of the great fort of Ravensburgh (near Hexton) confront the invaders.

Books Distributed by THE BOOK CASTLE

Pictorial Guide to Bedfordshire...Meadows/Larkman
The Story of Bedford...Godber
The Story of St.Albans...Toms
History of Milton Keynes, vol 1 ....Markham
History of Milton Keynes, vol ....Markham
Old Aylesbury...Viney/Nightingale

All the above are available via any bookshop, or from the publisher and bookseller
THE BOOK CASTLE , 12 Church Street Dunstable, Bedfordshire, LU5 4RU
Tel: (01582) 605670 Fax (01582) 662431 Email bc@book-castle.busclub.net

Treasures of the Chilterns

This 96-page book, published by the Chiltern Society, lists and describes some 250 places of interest to visit across the four counties of the Chilterns.

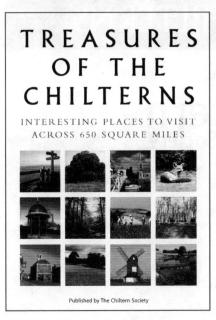

TREASURES
OF THE
CHILTERNS

INTERESTING PLACES TO VISIT
ACROSS 650 SQUARE MILES

Published by The Chiltern Society

Some of these places are well known, others are hidden away, but all are recommended by Society members who know the area well. Locations mentioned include the best places to view waterways, woodlands and wildlife. Great houses, villages and towns are detailed, and there is wide coverage of the area's notable churches, windmills and watermills. Some curiosities and original features of the Chilterns area are also listed in their own section. Map references are given for all locations, with full instructions on how to read them.

Printed in full colour and available from most good bookshops. Copies can be ordered by post from Chiltern Society Bookshop by Mail Order, 20 The Ridgeway, Watford, Herts WD17 4TN. For price details contact the Chiltern Society office on tel/fax: 01494 771250. The maps listed below are also available.

Chiltern Society Maps

1 High Wycombe & Marlow★
2 Henley & Nettlebed
3 Wendover & Princes Risborough★
4 Henley & Caversham
5 Sarratt & Chipperfield★
6 Amersham & Penn Country★
7 West Wycombe & Princes Risborough★
8 Chartridge & Cholesbury
9 Oxfordshire Escarpment★
10 Wallingford & Watlington★

11 The Hambleden Valley★
12 Hughenden Valley & Great Missenden
13 Beaconsfield & District★
14 Stokenchurch & Chinnor★
15 Crowmarsh & Nuffield
16 Goring & Mapledurham
17 Chesham & Berkhamsted
18 Tring & Wendover★
19 Ivinghoe & Ashridge★
20 Hemel Hempstead & the Gade Valley★

★Maps incorporating part of the Chiltern Way

The Chiltern
Society

We care for the Chilterns